Help!
My Social Life
is a Mess!

For Adrian, with love

Kathryn Lamb lives 'quietly' in Gillingham, Dorset, with her husband, Adrian Bovey, and their six children and two hamsters. Adrian has three teenage children.

Without the help of all these people (not so much the hamsters) she would have found it a lot more difficult to write this book. She would like to thank them all, including some very special grandparents.

Kathryn draws cartoons for *Private Eye* and *The Oldie*. She has illustrated a number of books for Piccadilly Press, and her first book, HELP! MY FAMILY IS DRIVING ME CRAZY! was extremely well-reviewed as well as being selected by *The Bookseller* as one of a hundred best books for Spring 1997 '. . . *it hits just the right humorous note.*'

A new book about school is in the pipeline.

Help! My Social Life is a Mess!

A SURVIVAL GUIDE FOR TEENAGERS

●

Kathryn Lamb

Piccadilly Press • London

Designed by Paul Cooper

Printed and bound by WBC, Bridgend
for the publishers, Piccadilly Press Ltd.
5 Castle Road, London NW1 8PR

A catalogue record of this book is available from the
British Library

ISBNs:1 85340 472 1 (hardback)
        1 85340 477 2 (trade paperback)

Contents

•Introduction

What is a 'social life'? Sometimes it seems like something everyone else has except you. Everyone else is getting ready to go out – and what happens to you? Not a lot. You are left staring fixedly at the television. Watching television is not really the best kind of social activity as it does not usually involve communicating with other people (except to say "Get out of the way!" or when your parents shout from the kitchen, "For God's sake, turn that television down!").

So what can you do? How can you improve your social life? You need FRIENDS. (This does not mean you should sit for hours in front of the television watching the programme *Friends*.) You need the warmth and companionship of REAL FRIENDS, who are very wonderful human beings indeed, without whom you would be completely lost. They are there to brighten your day (which sometimes means waking you up far too early in the morning when you are trying to catch up on lost sleep). They are there to add colour and pazzaz (yes, PAZZAZ!) to the rest of your day. They may even add woomph to your weekends, although it is debatable whether too much woomph is really a good idea. Your friends can also completely mess things up for you. You just wouldn't be without them. Would you?

Who's that boy?/Who's that girl?

Here are the main characters you will meet:

● Angelica Toogood

Angelica is nearly fifteen, and is the elder daughter of Mr and Mrs Toogood.

Mr Toogood is a bank manager, and Mrs Toogood is a housewife/homemaker and an expert cake-baker.

Angelica has an older brother, Grant, who is mega brainy and reads a lot of books. Her younger sister, Becky, is eleven, and she likes to try out Angelica's make-up and borrow her clothes.

KEY TO FAMILY TREE :

A   GRANDMA   B COLIN THE HAMSTER C BECKY

D   STANLEY THE CAT E MR TOOGOOD F GRANDPA

G GRANT TOOGOOD H MRS TOOGOOD I HORACE

J ANGELICA

● Basil Broke – Baz

Baz is fourteen and an only child, whose parents are divorced. He lives with his mother, Mrs Broke.

Every other weekend he stays with his father, Mr Broke, and his father's new wife, Celia. Celia has four children of

KEY TO FAMILY TREE :

  A BASIL BROKE ('BAZ') (HE'S INTO JAZZ)
  B 'FISH'
  C MRS BROKE

her own: Leonora, Theodora, Henrietta and William. Baz's father and Celia have recently had a baby, called Henry. The children make loads of noise, and Baz finds it hard to

KEY TO FAMILY TREE :
    A   MR BROKE, MRS CELIA BROKE and HOWLIN' HENRY
THE HALF-BROTHER   B   BASIL BROKE ('BAZ')   C   LEONORA, THEODORA
AND HENRIETTA   D   WILLIAM   E   MR and MRS RABBIT

get enough sleep. Baz blames his father for the fact that his mother is always broke, and has to go out to work (in a fish shop). However, his father pays for Baz's saxophone lessons.

● Soumik Sen

Soumik is thirteen. He is an only child with two doting parents, and many relations. There are frequent family gatherings, which Soumik does not enjoy, since his girl cousins (there are eighteen of them) tend to whisper together and giggle a lot. As the only boy, he is the focus of everyone's attention.

KEY TO FAMILY TREE :

A   SOUMIK SEN

B   MR AND MRS SEN

C   AUNT ANEENA AND HER 2 DAUGHTERS
D   AUNT SITA AND HER 5 DAUGHTERS
E   AUNT PRITI AND HER 4 DAUGHTERS
F   AUNT JASMEENA AND HER 6 DAUGHTERS

● Steve Cash

Steve is fifteen. His parents run their own businesses, and they are too busy most of the time to take much notice of Steve, or his younger brother, James (thirteen).

Steve has formed his own band, and he frequently upsets the neighbours by making too much noise. He thinks he is pretty cool, but he sometimes feels lonely, and Baz is his only real friend.

KEY TO FAMILY TREE :

A STEVE CASH   B JAMES CASH

C MR CASH   D MRS CASH

● Amy Average

Amy is fourteen. Her little brother, Anthony, is eight. Mr Average is currently out of work, so the family derives its income from Mrs Average's job as a music teacher.

Angelica and Amy are best friends (except when they fall out).

KEY TO FAMILY TREE :

A   AMY   B   ANTHONY ('PEST')   C   GRAN

D   MR AVERAGE   E   MRS AVERAGE

F   'SQUAWK' THE PARROT

CHAPTER 1
Your Friends and Your Social Life

WHAT IS A FRIEND?

A friend is someone who is there when you need them (except when they've gone out). A friend is someone you can talk to (except when all *they* can talk about is their new boyfriend/girlfriend). A friend is someone who will listen (occasionally), someone you can laugh with (except when they're in a bad mood), and someone on whose shoulder you can cry (but not if they're wearing the new jacket they've just spent all their money on). Friends provide a refuge/somewhere to go when things are not going so well

FRIENDS

at home. (But don't be surprised if things are even worse at the friend's house, so you end up going back to *your* home, to comfort *them*.)

Friends fall into several categories (they also have a tendency to *fall out* of several categories):

1) BEST
2) BOSSY
3) BABYISH
4) BRIGHT AND BEAUTIFUL AND BRILLIANT
5) BORING
6) YOU THINK THEY ARE YOUR FRIEND, AND THEN FIND OUT THEY AREN'T
7) THE HANGING ON 'FRIEND'

How do you know what kind of friend you've got? Answer the following questions to find out!

QUESTION ONE: You are trying on a pair of trousers in the changing room at your favourite shop. Unfortunately, a button flies off and the seam splits right down the leg when you attempt to do them up. Your friend is with you at the time. What is their reaction?

a) Hysterical laughter. You feel embarrassed, and tell them to shut up, but after a few minutes find yourself equally helpless with mirth.

b) "OH MY GOD! YOU'VE REALLY PUT ON WEIGHT, HAVEN'T YOU? YOU'RE GOING TO

HAVE TO SHOW THEM WHAT YOU'VE DONE! YOU'LL HAVE TO PAY FOR IT, YOU KNOW. I'M GLAD I'M NOT IN YOUR SHOES!" All this is said in a loud and clearly audible voice so that when you emerge from the changing room you find that everyone in the shop is staring in your direction.

c) "Oh dear." This is all they say. They just stand and stare hard at you and at the offending trousers. They may then say something like, "I don't think they fit."

d) They look at you with an expression of mingled fear and embarrassment, as if you have done this on purpose. Their bottom lip trembles. They say, in a whisper, "I wish Mum was here. She'd know what to do."

e) "Don't worry. Look, I'll sort this out for you. Give me the trousers. They're obviously badly made. They shouldn't sell clothes which fall apart as easily as that. I'll show them what's happened, and I'm sure they won't make a fuss. Would you like me to bring you a larger size? I might try some on, too."

f) "I TOLD YOU NOT TO TRY THOSE TROUSERS. I TOLD YOU THEY WEREN'T RIGHT FOR YOU. NOW DO YOU BELIEVE ME? NOW WILL YOU TRY THOSE AMAZING WHITE AND GOLD FLARES I WANTED YOU TO TRY IN THE FIRST PLACE? YOU'VE JUST *GOT* TO GET THEM! THEY'RE *YOU*!"

g) Your friend hasn't even noticed the trouser incident. They have chosen a grey sweatshirt to try on, and have been standing motionless staring at their reflection for the last half-hour. The shop assistant asks them if they are all right. Your friend mumbles something about "not quite the right shade of grey." You seize the opportunity to sneak out and stuff the wrong trousers back on the rack.

ANSWERS TO QUESTION ONE:

a) Best friend. This is the friend you can most easily laugh with, even when (or especially when) things are not going your way. They may not have all the answers, but they usually cheer you up, and make you feel better. They help you to see the funny side.

b) Someone who delights in embarrassing you in public, no matter how upset they can see you are, is not your friend at all.

c) The Hanging On Friend has nothing much to say, and gives very little.

d) Babyish friend. A shopping expedition with this friend is likely to end in tears. In fact, almost everything will.

e) Bright and beautiful and brilliant. This friend knows exactly what to do and say, in any situation. But they make you feel slightly useless. And when they try on clothes they inevitably look better in them than you do.

f) Bossy friend. This person always knows what's best for you (or they think they do).

g) Boring friend. It is sometimes their complete self-absorption which makes them boring. They don't need a friend, they just need a mirror/television/wall to stare at.

QUESTION TWO: You borrow your friend's best shirt and spill ink/coffee/tea all over it. What is their reaction?

a) "It really doesn't matter. Forget it. Can I borrow your white trousers?" So you lend them your white trousers, only to have them returned the following day covered in mud, tomato sauce and unidentifiable awfulness, and ripped in several places.

b) "OH, YOU STUPID IDIOT!" However, after a brief burst of anger they quickly accept your apology and your offers to help remove the stain.

c) "Oh dear." Followed by, "I don't think you meant to do that."

d) "I TOLD YOU NOT TO SHAKE THAT PEN/ SAUCE BOTTLE – I TOLD YOU TOO MUCH TEA/ COFFEE IS BAD FOR YOU, NOW LOOK WHAT IT'S DONE TO MY SHIRT! GO AND SOAK IT IN A LUKEWARM SOLUTION OF WATER, VINEGAR AND BAKING SODA FOR TWENTY MINUTES, THEN PUT IT THROUGH A COOL WASH, THEN

REPEAT THE PROCESS, THEN RESHAPE WHILE DAMP, AND WHEN YOU'VE DONE THAT YOU'LL PROBABLY HAVE TO BLEACH IT . . ."

e) "Muuuuuum! Muuuuuum! She's ruined my best shirt! It's not fair! I hate you! What am I going to wear to the Teddy Bears' Picnic now? Boo hoooooooooo!"

BABYISH FRIEND

f) "Oh, don't worry about it! You can keep the shirt, if you like. If you give me eighteen pounds I'll just buy a new one. Oh, really? You don't have that much money? Poor you! No wonder you always look so . . . Oh, sorry, I didn't mean to say that. You look wonderful. Really. Just forget it. It doesn't matter."

g) "That's my best grey shirt. Never mind. I can wear my school shirt instead. I really like our school uniform."

ANSWERS TO QUESTION TWO:

a) The person who is nice to your face, and then takes revenge behind your back, is not your friend at all.

b) Best friend. It is the sign of a close friendship when you fall out from time to time, but only briefly, and forgiveness is never far away. You feel relaxed enough with each other to express your feelings, both good and bad.

c) The Hanging On Friend is not renowned for their helpful comments. They will simply hang around and mention the shirt incident at intervals, as if they have nothing else to talk about (which may or may not be true).

d) Bossy friend. This kind of friend is an expert at the 'I-told-you-so' approach.

e) Babyish friend. If you upset this friend, he or she will sulk and refuse to talk to you for weeks, which will probably come as a great relief.

f) Beware the bright and beautiful and brilliant friend. They can also be the bitchy friend. They probably don't care if they upset you or lose your friendship, because they have so many other friends and admirers.

g) Boring friend. You are unlikely to have a bad reaction from this friend. In fact, you are unlikely to have any reaction at all.

FRIENDS AGAIN (now that the trouser and shirt incidents are over).

1) BEST FRIEND

This is the person you feel closest to, because you confide in them, and you tell each other how you feel. However, this is also the friend you are most likely to fall out with:

● The scene

Amy and Angelica have spent the whole day together, and Amy is sleeping over at Angelica's house. Amy has been singing her favourite song by the Nut Girls all day, and she is still singing it at eleven o'clock at night. Suddenly Angelica snaps. "Will you stop singing that stupid song? You sound like a stuck pig. Do you really think you can sing or something?" There is a profound silence. Then Amy says, "Well, thanks. I thought you were my friend. Anyway, you've been sniffing all day, and it's really beginning to get to me. Why don't you blow your nose? It's big enough." Another profound silence. This time the silence goes for longer. How do you break it?

● Bad way to break the silence: "By the way, Amy, Scott doesn't like you. He told me you

remind him of a rabbit. Because of your teeth." This is known as 'adding insult to injury' and will only succeed in making the silence longer and even colder. In fact, the temperature in the girls' bedroom has now sunk to an all-time low, and frost is forming on the window panes.

● Better way to break the silence:

"Er, it's a bit quiet in here, isn't it? Look, Amy, I really don't want to fall out with you. If you like, I'll put the Nut Girls on my stereo, and we can both sing along! But I'm warning you, my singing's really bad!" If you admit to some faults of your own, it will make the other person feel better. Then you should be able to laugh together again.

● Best way to break the silence:

"I'm sorry." This can be very hard to say, but once you've said it you will feel a renewed warmth, and you can enjoy your friendship again. With a best friend, you may both find yourselves saying "I'm sorry" at almost the same moment, because you know that your friendship is too important to let it fall apart over some small matter.

2) BOSSY FRIEND

This kind of friend is a bit of a know-it-all; but do they really know it all? Friends like this have a habit of suggesting you do things that *they* would never do. Perhaps they are curious to see what happens, but too cowardly to do it themselves.

● The scene

Amy has for a long time been secretly, or not so secretly, in love with Baz. She confides in a girl called Belinda Bossington-Boots, who tries to persuade her to do something about it. "You have GOT to tell him how you feel!" she says. "Or he will never know. Write him a note and push it through his door. GO ON!"

● What should Amy do?: She should ask

herself *why* Belinda is so keen that she should do this. Would Belinda herself have the nerve to do it? If the answer is probably no, then Amy should definitely question Belinda's motives. It is as if Belinda is just winding up the situation for her own entertainment, not out of any real friendship for Amy. A real friend would understand Amy's reluctance, and leave her to make up her own mind, without putting pressure on her.

● What Amy actually does: She writes

the note (Belinda tells her what to say), and pushes it through Baz's door. (She does this more to please Belinda than because she really thinks it is a good idea.) The door is opened by Baz's mother.

"Oh, er, hi, Mrs Broke! That's a . . . a letter for Baz!"

"Oh, thanks, Amy. I'll give it to him. He's got his girl-friend here at the moment. Would you like to come in?"

"Um, I, er, that is, NO. See you!" Amy retreats at high speed, her face burning with embarrassment. She has just decided to kill Belinda.

3) BABYISH FRIEND

● The scene

Amy is spending the day with a friend from school called
Claire. Claire is thirteen and likes the same music as Amy.
What Amy was not prepared for was Claire's extensive
collection of Sylvanian Family toys. Her whole bedroom is
devoted to them. She has turned it into an entire miniature
village, peopled by tiny toy animals with names like Rose
Timbertop, Misty Waters and Breezy Babblebrook.

"Er, I think Baz and Scott are outside playing football,"

says Amy. "They're really great guys, aren't they? Baz is cool. So's Scott. He's a hunk. Which one do you like?"

Claire looks blankly at Amy. "But we can't go out now. Lavender and Larkspur, the baby rabbit twins, have got a new playpen and mobile for their nursery. We have to look after them because their parents have gone out for a drive in their car."

"Er . . . they're toys, Claire. They'll be all right without us."

Claire sounds a little upset. "Yes, but . . . don't you like them?"

WHAT SHOULD AMY DO NEXT?

● **Bad thing to say:** "You're sad, Claire." This is unkind. Just because your friend is taking longer than you to grow up is no reason to hurt their feelings.

● **Better thing to say:** "I need some fresh air. Shall we go for a walk?" Don't challenge them by insisting that they have to share your interest in members of the opposite sex, otherwise you will turn into a bossy friend. Don't exclude them either. Perhaps they've just lacked the opportunity to go out and meet people and widen their horizons. They might need your help and encouragement, or they might not − if they are not ready to move on then leave them where they are.

4) BRIGHT AND BEAUTIFUL AND BRILLIANT FRIEND

● The scene

Jemima Proudfoot (Arabella Proudfoot's older and even more beautiful sister) has invited Angelica to go to a party with her. Angelica feels really pleased, because Jemima is so popular, and she is proud of the fact that Jemima has chosen *her* as a friend. Jemima looks wonderful in a cut-off top and spray-on black miniskirt which shows off her fantastic figure. Angelica suddenly regrets having chosen to wear her tightest black dress which shows off the fact that she has been bingeing on Microchips and Extended Energy Mars bars (twice the size of a normal Mars bar) recently, and has acquired an 'extended' waistline.

BRIGHT AND BEAUTIFUL AND BRILLIANT FRIEND

"You've got such a lovely, curvy figure, Angelica!" says Jemima, kindly (patronisingly? Angelica is not quite sure).

All the guys at the party flock round Jemima like bees round a honeypot, and Angelica finds herself totally ignored. She feels a little used, as though she has only been taken along to the party to provide a contrast to Jemima's beauty, radiance and sparkle, etc.

What is the best thing to do in this situation?

● *Not* the best thing to do: Don't try to compete with the bright and beautiful one. Don't stand beside them like a lemon (a lemon beside an exotic fruit), attempting to sparkle. It is difficult to sparkle convincingly when no one is showing any interest in you at all. No one seems to notice your sparkling wit, and you end up feeling like a non-sparkling twit. (You can practise sparkling in a mirror if you like, but the effect is likely to be extraordinary, as if you are suffering from multiple nervous twitches. It is not worth it. Your time to sparkle will come, if you just stop worrying about it.)

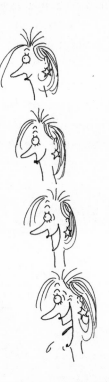

YOU CAN PRACTISE ' SPARKLING '...

● The best thing to do: Put as much distance as you can between yourself and the bright and beautiful one. Then you can just be yourself, rather than someone else's disconsolate shadow. You may end up having a better time, possibly making just one good friend, while they flit around like the proverbial butterfly, unable to settle anywhere for long. Remember: it is not easy being beautiful (no one is quite sure why, but this is meant to be a comforting thought for most of us).

5) BORING FRIEND

● The scene

Baz has gone round to his friend Herm's house. No one knows for certain why Herm is called Herm.

There are several possible reasons:

1) It is short for Herman. In which case his parents are to blame for coming up with such an awful name, guaranteed to give their son a difficult start in life. His mother probably named him after the lead singer of Herman's Hermits, a popular singing group in the 60s.

2) Herm is short for Hermit, which is appropriate, since Herm never goes out.

3) It is a nickname derived from the fact that Herman's only utterance, when anyone asks him a question, is "Errm . . ." which comes out as "Herm" when he clears his throat at the same time. He is not known to say anything very much apart from this.

Baz likes to go round to Herm's house to chill out. But after a while he begins to feel so chilled out he wonders if

Herm is still alive. So what do you do if you have an intensely boring friend?

● **First thing to do**: Check the boring friend's pulse or listen to their heart. If it is still beating, move on to the:

● **Second thing to do**: Try to tempt them to do something or go out somewhere. Again, it may be lack of opportunity or basic lack of confidence which has made them so boring. Given a chance and loads of encouragement they may turn out to be a bundle of fun. Or not. It is always worth a try.

BORING FRIEND

6) YOU THINK THEY ARE YOUR FRIEND, AND THEN FIND OUT THEY AREN'T

● The scene

Amy thinks she has found a new best friend, whose name is Heather. Heather likes the same music, the same clothes, the same people . . . Heather encourages Amy to tell her who she fancies at school, and Amy lets on that she is in love with Baz. Baz already has a girlfriend at the school, whose name is Judy. One day Amy finds herself confronted by Judy, who, in front of everyone, tells her in no uncertain terms that Baz is not, and never will be, interested in Amy, so why doesn't she just go away and "get a life" of her own? Amy feels awful, and deeply embarrassed. How did Judy know? Then, with a sinking feeling, she realises . . . Heather has been spreading rumours behind her back, and telling people her secrets.

● What Amy would like to say to Heather: This is probably unprintable. It is very hurtful when you have trusted someone and been let down by them. But it is probably better not to lose your temper with them, because they are really not worth it. Don't give them the satisfaction of knowing that they have upset you. If you're very upset, talk to a real friend about it. Just because this friend has let you down, not all of them will.

● What Amy should say to Heather: "I don't think you should have upset Judy

like that, Heather. What I told you was meant to be just between us. I hope you won't do anything like that again." In other words, without losing her temper, Amy can make the point that Heather has not behaved like a friend. If there is any good in Heather (and there is in most people) she will probably feel sorry, especially since Amy is behaving towards her in a reasonable manner, avoiding any further nastiness.

7) THE HANGING ON FRIEND

● The scene

You know the saying "Two's company, three's a crowd"? The hanging on 'friend' has never heard of this saying. They follow you around everywhere, even when you are trying to have a quiet conversation with a friend, or you are with the boy/girl you particularly like. There they are

THE HANGING ON FRIEND

again. They don't usually say very much, or even do anything in particular. They just hang around looking as though they are waiting for something to happen, which never does. They make you feel uncomfortable.

● **What you would like to say to this 'friend':** "GO AWAY AND GET A LIFE OF YOUR OWN!"

● **What could you say to them?:** "I've decided to take up free-fall parachuting. Want to come along?" The really determined hanger-on will follow you anywhere, even out of an aeroplane hundreds of thousands of metres up in the air. So this may not work. Find out first if there is something they really *don't* like, such as work. Then declare your intention of carrying out extra studies in the school library and at home, and that you must on no account be disturbed. If they still hang around you, tell them that the sound of their breathing is disturbing your concentration. Make yourself so incredibly boring that they will probably go and find someone more interesting to hang around. Alternatively, you could go jogging, put on a sudden burst of speed, hide behind a tree, and lose them that way. All of these are rather extreme measures, of course.

● **A better solution:** This is actually to have a quiet chat with the hanger-on, and find out, if you can, what their problem is. They may have very little confidence and no real friends of their own, so that they latch on to others and follow them around to avoid being bored. If they really are very lonely, invite them to come round one day, and you could go for a wander round the shops, or to the park. On their own (rather than hanging round you and your friends) they might feel encouraged to open up a little, and turn out to be better than you thought. You can also explain, as gently as you can, that you enjoy talking to them on their own, but that you also enjoy doing this with your other friends, so would they mind leaving you alone in future if they see you are busy? In other words, make your feelings clear, but do it gently. There is nothing to be gained by humiliating a probably insecure person in front of other people.

PROBLEM ONE: Going out with the crowd

● The scene

Soumik, Baz, Steve, Angelica, Amy and Becky have gone to the cinema. Steve starts a popcorn fight. Soon they're all throwing popcorn at each other. Angelica shrieks with laughter. Unfortunately the people in the next row aren't so amused when popcorn goes down the back of their necks. One of the advertisements showing on the screen has loud rock music. Steve gets up, stands on his seat and plays the air guitar. "Get down, you idiot!" hisses Baz. Since Steve is wearing his shades, and it is rather dark in the cinema, he can't actually see his feet. He loses his footing and falls with a terrific thump on to the floor, where he lies under his friends' feet. "Can't see a thing!" he shouts. "What's happened to the screen?" At this point one of the cinema attendants tells them that they'll all have to leave if they can't be quiet. Steve gets up, stands to attention and gives a military-style salute when the attendant's back is turned.

WHAT SHOULD YOU DO WHEN A MEMBER OF THE CROWD YOU'RE IN STARTS ACTING UP?

● **Bad thing to do:** Encourage them to be even sillier by laughing, and calling out to them. Then, when there's any kind of trouble as a result of their behaviour, pretend you have nothing to do with them, and you've never met them before in your life. This is most unfair of course, and you are not being a good friend.

● **Better thing to do:** Tell them to shut up, and stop being such an idiot. This is all right, but you may not want to be seen as completely boring and more like your parents than your parents.

● **Best things to do:**

1) Ignore them. (Difficult of course when, for instance, someone is wearing three hats at once, has two corks stuffed up their nostrils and is doing an impression of an orang-utan on heat.) They are looking for an audience so that they can be the centre of attention. This is OK for a short while, but it can get very boring when one person demands endless attention.

PRETEND NOT TO NOTICE WHAT THEY'RE DOING

2) Alternatively, you can try distracting them by saying you like what they're wearing, and where did they get it, and so on. If they are an attention-seeker, they will welcome questions about themselves.

GOOD THINGS ABOUT GOING OUT WITH THE CROWD:

1) It is fun going out with a lot of friends.
2) You may feel more confident as part of a crowd. There is strength in numbers.
3) You feel proud to 'belong' to a crowd of friends since it is like a proof of popularity.

BAD THINGS ABOUT GOING OUT WITH THE CROWD:

1) You may get carried away and feel tempted to indulge in antisocial behaviour – such as an out-of-control popcorn fight in a crowded cinema. Other people will get angry – not unreasonably.

2) There is strength in numbers. But NEVER use that strength to intimidate other people.

3) If the rest of the crowd is urging you to do something you are not sure about, ask yourself if it is something you would do if you were on your own. If the answer is "No" then don't do it.

PROBLEM TWO: When your friends have different interests to you

● The scene

Baz keeps raving on about a motorbike which he has been helping some older boys to take to bits and build again. He is suddenly totally fascinated by motorbikes and anything to do with motorbikes. He has covered one wall of his room (it is not a very big room) with the most enormous poster of a motorbike that Amy has ever seen. She has gone to his house for a chat and to ask his advice about some maths homework. (Yes, you're right – this is an *excuse* to get close to him because she has always fancied him.)

What Amy hopes that Baz will say next is, "Anyway, that's enough about me and bikes. How're things with you, Amy?"

What Baz actually says next is, "Yeah, so then we attached the spare widget to the multifunctional transponder and the thing just roared – I mean, it really roared! We all jumped out of our skins but Steve said that it wasn't making the right noise. So we had to take it all to bits again."

● **What is happening to Amy?:** Her brain has gone into cold storage, her eyelids are drooping, she is fighting to stay awake. She stifles an enormous yawn.

● **What Amy should not say:** "Oh, stop waffling on about stupid motorbikes! Can't you think about anything else?" This head-on tactless approach will only succeed in alienating someone she would still like to be friends with (or rather more than friends with).

● **What Amy could say:** "Your motorbike sounds really cool. I'd like to see it one of these days. Oh, and by the way, did you know I've got tickets for a concert by the Old Spice Boyz on 24 March? Would you like to come? What do you think of their music by the way? Can we put something on your stereo? What would you like to listen to? Go on – you choose. Do you like my hair, by the way? I had it feathered – I hope you don't think that I look like a chicken, ha ha ha – that's a joke, by the way. Oh, and I'm sorry to be really boring but can you help me with this maths homework? You're really good at maths. I wish I was. What did you think of Mr Truscott's red trousers? He looked so funny. We were in fits!"

WHEN YOUR FRIENDS HAVE DIFFERENT
INTERESTS TO YOU

This is more tactful. It also guarantees that Baz cannot get a word in about motorbikes – or anything else. It is his turn to acquire a glazed look.

● **The best approach:** It is probably best to be tactful and show an interest in whatever fascinates your friend. You can then ask questions which might help to steer your friend's mind in other directions which might be of interest to both of you. Give them time to reply to these questions, and hopefully you will get more out of them than a one-word answer. If you show an interest in them, they should show an interest in you. If they don't, ask yourself if you really need them as a friend.

PROBLEM THREE: When your friends have more, or less, money than you

● The scene

Steve and Baz are looking around a hi-fi and music store together. Steve buys a couple of CDs and a new set of expensive headphones. Baz sees a CD he has wanted for ages but can't afford to buy. He knows that Steve has plenty of cash, and he feels envious. What should he do?

● Bad thing to do: Borrow money. This is a recipe for disaster in a friendship, especially if you know you can't afford to pay it back. You may have a generous friend, but it is not fair to put a strain on the friendship by taking advantage of their generosity repeatedly. They will inevitably begin to feel that you are using them to get what you want, and they will feel resentful. If you are going to borrow money, you must be absolutely certain that you can pay it back, and must do so as soon as possible. Otherwise, you may end up with all sorts of things (CDs, clothes, make-up etc.) but you will have lost something rather more valuable – a friend. Similarly, if you have more money than your friend, you should not feel guilty or obliged to spend your money on them too often.

● Better thing to do: Share your friend's enjoyment of whatever things they have bought (likewise share whatever you have bought with your friend). You can listen to the new CDs together, and you can exchange clothes and make-up. Whether you have money or not, it

SPOT THE DIFFERENCE

is unlikely that you won't have something your friend would appreciate borrowing or sharing.

● **Best thing to do:** Relax, and remember that you can't buy friendship. That way you should avoid feelings of jealousy or of being used.

SOME OTHER FRIENDS WHO YOU (PROBABLY) DON'T NEED:

1) The friend who *thinks* she or he is good at hairdressing.

If you have a friend who has a natural flair for hair or who has had the proper training, then lucky you. But not

41

so lucky you if you have a friend who gets a strange gleam in her (usually *her*) eyes when she gets hold of a pair of scissors. "Come here," she cries. "You'd look great with your hair feathered. I know how to do it. I can save you a fortune!"

DO NOT let her do it. You will look like a chicken. She will definitely NOT save you a fortune because you will have to pay a professional hairdresser to put your friend's mistakes right. At the very worst, you will end up having to have all your hair cut off and start again.

YOU WILL LOOK
LIKE A CHICKEN

2) The friend who thinks she or he is good at ear-piercing.

You need this friend like you need a hole in the head (or a hole in the ear, ha ha ha). Always go to a professional beautician or jeweller.

●CHAPTER 2
Boyfriends/ Girlfriends

Like parties and 'fun' in general, you may sometimes feel that a boyfriend/girlfriend is something that everyone else has except you. This isn't really the case, although it is true that some people seem to have an endless stream of admirers (doesn't that sort of person just make you sick?). Don't worry – Mr or Ms Right will come along eventually, although it may feel about a thousand times worse than waiting for a bus (and then of course, two come along at once – life can be very complicated).

WHAT IS A BOYFRIEND/GIRLFRIEND?

It seems to be someone you 'go out' with on a regular basis, although you can just as well stay in with them. However, people usually ask you whether you are going out with anyone. They don't usually say, "Are you staying in with anyone?"

PROBLEM ONE: What to do when no one seems to notice you

● The scene

Amy has been to two parties recently, at both of which she has noticed a really fantastic groovy guy. But he never seems to look in her direction. She knows he is going to

Steve's next party, and she manages to get herself invited as well. Her parents say she can go as long as Grant Toogood goes along to look after her. They like Grant, and keep hoping that he and Amy will become good friends. Unfortunately, Amy thinks that Grant is a complete dork and all gangly. She is quite rude to him, although he is always pleasant to her.

WHAT CAN AMY DO TO ATTRACT THE ATTENTION OF THE BOY SHE LIKES?

1) She can dye her hair an eye-catching shade of haystack blonde or flaming red (green would also be eye-catching, but would be more likely to put him off).

2) She can use dramatic make-up, like luminous lipstick and nail varnish which will show up well in the dark at a disco.

3) She can wear her brightest, slinkiest clothes, and a cool hat.

4) She can use half a bottle of perfume so that he cannot possibly fail to notice how wonderful she smells.

5) She can practise the Dance of the Seven Veils, or something similar – anyway, the sort of dance that women do in the mystic East to drive men wild.

Amy decides to do all of these. She also decides to wear a pair of dark glasses to make her look mysterious and sultry.

However, she has to take these off since she keeps walking into people at the party.

And there he is! But before she has a chance to so much as pout or pucker (attractively, she hopes – she has been practising puckering in the mirror) in his direction, Kevin Winterbotham, the disco dork, taps her on the

PRACTISING PUCKERING IN THE MIRROR

shoulder. "Wow!" he exclaims, as she turns to confront him. "You're a well sexy babe, some cool chick, huh? Wanna dance?"

KEVIN WINTERBOTHAM, THE DISCO DORK, TAPS HER ON THE SHOULDER

"No," says Amy, but it is too late. Kevin's arms, which are twice as long as they should be, are already wrapped round her. She struggles to prise them off.

Suddenly Grant Toogood is there. "Hey, Kev!" he says. "I don't think Amy wants to dance with you. Leave her alone, will you?" Kevin shrugs and waddles away (he is part disco dork, part disco duck). Amy looks at Grant in a new light. He is her hero! The other boy is forgotten, and Amy and Grant dance together for the rest of the evening.

MY HERO!

All of this proves nothing, really, except that you never know what's going to happen next in life, and you cannot really plan your romantic life like you would plan to do the shopping.

PROBLEM TWO: Asking a boy/girl out in the first place. How do you do it?

● The scene

Amy wants to ask Baz to go to a film with her. She likes the idea of sitting next to him in the dark for an hour and a half, and wonders whether it might be the start of a wonderful relationship. But she feels awkward and nervous. How should she approach the situation?

● Not the right way to approach

it: This is to deliberately look scruffy and not particularly

46

bothered about anything, including her appearance, and say something like: "Oh, by the way, there's a film on and I was thinking of going to see it. I don't know if it's any good, so I don't suppose you'd want to see it." This approach almost guarantees the answer "Not really". Appearing overly casual and not bothered at all is a kind of self-protection because you are not giving away anything of yourself, such as the fact that you care. But it is most unlikely that the other person will want to go out with you if you show absolutely no enthusiasm for their company whatsoever.

● **A not much better way to approach it:** Of course, you can go too far the other way and put someone off by coming on too strong. It is probably not a good idea to launch straight into something akin to the balcony scene in *Romeo and Juliet*, with a carefully-rehearsed speech, along the lines of: "Wherefore hath thou been all my life, oh my love, and wilt thou come unto the cinema with me?" Don't rehearse too much what you are going to say to the other person, or your little speech will come out sounding deeply unnatural, with all the wrong expression in all the wrong places.

● **The best way to approach it:** Remember that the person you are asking out is human, like you. They are likely to be flattered that you want to go out with them. They are most unlikely to say something like, "Oh my God, NO! I'd rather wrestle with a wild bear in the desolate wastes of Siberia than go out with YOU!" So relax. Brush your hair, put on your best smile (this does not mean a cheesy grin), and think of something that the other person would probably like to do. Choose a film that you are reasonably certain they would enjoy (if you are asking a motorbike-mad rugby player out for the first time, *The Railway Children* may not be the best choice). Make it sound as if you were going anyway (which offers you some protection from feeling a complete fool), but balance it by saying something like, "I'd really like it if you could come along." The other person will then feel encouraged, but not pressurised.

● **And another thing . . . :** Remember that you can be friends with a boy or a girl without pushing the friendship into a boyfriend/girlfriend situation. If you approach every friendship with a member of the opposite sex as if it is a potential Great Romance, you are unlikely to relax and just be yourself. Some of the best romances grow out of a long-term friendship, so it is a good idea to enjoy and appreciate your whole circle of friends (the 'gang') without feeling you *have* to concentrate exclusively on one person.

PROBLEM THREE: What to do with the boyfriend/girlfriend once you've got them

You have two options, really. You either go out or you stay in.

REASONS FOR GOING OUT:

1) To be seen. You want the world to know that you're going out with this good-looking guy/cool babe.

2) To get away from parents, siblings and other relations, who tend to stare at you and ask silly questions. Offer to walk the dog, anything to get you out of the house. Tell them you're going skateboarding. Tell them you're taking the dog skateboarding.

TELL THEM YOU'RE TAKING THE DOG SKATEBOARDING

3) To do 'something', such as take in a film. Unfortunately, this costs money, which is something you may not have. You can earn some by washing the car (or washing the dog) or you can do something fun that costs nothing (like playing on the swings in the park and pretending you're both still ten!).

REASONS FOR STAYING IN:

1) No money. Watching the movie on television and raiding the fridge costs you nothing, but you should always ask your parent's permission to have a friend round. Clear it with them first as to what exactly is on offer and what isn't (in the fridge and on the television, and anywhere else). Always obey the house rules. And remember that it may be daunting for both the boyfriend/girlfriend and your parents to meet each other for the first time. Take things gently. Make everyone a cup of coffee/tea.

2) The sofa is comfortable, and it is nice to sit on it next to someone you love. You can watch a video, if there is one. You may find it a little difficult to keep your cool if your boyfriend loves scary films and you don't. You try desperately to appear casual and mildly amused when you are scared witless. Why not tell him you're terrified? Perhaps he will put a protective arm round your shoulders.

If he doesn't, go and make some sandwiches or something. On the other hand, even if you love weepies, it is probably not a good idea to get through an entire box of Kleenex and then blow your nose on the sleeve of his T-shirt. You end up looking red-eyed, red-nosed and not an appealing sight. And it is probably not his sort of film, anyway.

Also, beware of enthusing too much over the gorgeous actor/actress. When you have said for the tenth time, "Hasn't Brad got a terrific body?" your boyfriend may begin to feel intimidated. And he is unlikely to agree with you. Similarly, if you are a boy, it is somewhat tactless to exclaim at the size of your favourite actress's bikini-clad silicon implants more than five times (in five minutes), especially if your girlfriend tends to disappear when she turns sideways.

3) You want to show them your dog/cat/hamster, your collection of cool hats, your photograph albums, and so on. However, don't go into overkill, or you'll bore them to death (they may not find you as fascinating as you find yourself).

4) Listening to music.

THINGS TO SAY WHEN YOU GO OUT (OR STAY IN)

● Good things to say:

1) "Hello. Your hair looks great."

2) "Have you heard the new single by the Nut Girls?" (or other well-known group).

3) "It's really great to see you again."

● Bad things to say:

1) "You're late. You didn't phone me. What's happened to your hair?"

2) "What's that smell?" (*Don't* say this – it is a question guaranteed to prey on someone's deepest insecurities, and you will find the other person surreptitiously sniffing their armpits.)

3) "Yawn. Yawn. Yawn." Don't YAWN endlessly in someone else's company, no matter how tired you are. You will make them feel utterly boring. And don't yawn down the phone.

4) "You look just like your mum/dad/uncle Fred."

You will find that after a few dates it will get easier to know what to say. You will think of more and more things you really want to say to the other person and, with any luck, they will feel the same.

PROBLEM FOUR: How to end it, and how to deal with it when they end it

● The scene

Angelica has done everything she can to attract Mark Merton, and it has worked. He has asked her out several times and they have had some laughs together. But having done so much to attract him, she now wishes she hadn't, because William Warmwell has asked her out. She doesn't want to hurt Mark's feelings, but she really wants to go out with William. She has decided that Mark is a sweet guy but not her type.

HOW NOT TO HURT THEIR FEELINGS:

1) Don't mention that there is someone else whose company you prefer. Just say you wish to cool it.

2) Don't criticise them. If you are about to reject them, there is no need to add insult to injury by telling them what you don't like about them. Instead, tell them you have had a really great time with them, which you will always remember, but that you feel you need some time on your own.

3) If you have said any of the above things, it would be pretty unfeeling to flaunt the replacement boy-friend/girlfriend all over the place the very next day. So take things gradually (probably a good idea anyway), and don't go out too much for a while, or you may find yourself in a difficult situation.

● **The scene**

Steve and Angelica have been out together on several dates. They have also spent their weekends sitting in their favourite café, drinking coffee and eating the occasional bag of crisps and packet of biscuits. On the next Saturday Angelica wanders into the café, looking for Steve. She finds him. But he is not alone. He is sitting at a table with Jemima Proudfoot, and they are both tucking into the most enormous breakfast ever seen (bacon, egg, sausage, mushrooms, fried bread – the works). Steve NEVER bought Angelica such a breakfast. In fact, the most he ever bought her was a bag of cheese and onion crisps and a packet of cookies.

Angelica stares at them in complete horror. She feels like being sick on the spot. What should she do?

● **Bad thing to do:** Take Jemima's full English breakfast and empty the plate over her head and into her lap. This tactic will achieve very little, and it is Angelica, not Jemima, who is likely to end up with egg on her face. Everyone else in the café will be laughing at her, which will make her feel worse, and Steve will be angry with her. Jemima will be full of righteous indignation, and will probably send her a bill for dry-cleaning. She should also remember that it is Steve who has actually betrayed her.

BAD THING TO DO

● **Even worse thing to do:** This is to shout at Steve and tell him in no uncertain terms what she thinks of him. This reaction will serve only to reveal her vulnerability, and she will then have to turn and walk out of the café with everyone staring at her. It will take a long time to live this down.

● **Better thing to do**: Say, "Do you mind if I join you?" and sit down beside them with a cup of coffee and a pack of biscuits. She can be perfectly friendly and polite, and inwardly have the satisfaction of knowing that she has completely put them off their breakfast.

● **Best thing to do**: Quietly turn and walk away. A dignified departure from the scene speaks volumes and should make Steve feel small for behaving like a Complete Pig.

HOW NOT TO GET HURT:

1) Beware of taking any relationship *too* seriously until and unless you are a hundred per cent certain that the other person feels the same way about you. Steer well clear of one-sided relationships, particularly if you are always having to do things to please the other person, or retain their interest. This will sap your confidence and the relationship is unlikely to work despite your efforts.

2) A sense of humour is essential. It is nice to laugh together, even if you're no longer going out. Why should it be all or nothing? Just because you've cooled it, doesn't mean you can't still be friends. You can laugh on your own as well, and it doesn't necessarily mean you've gone mad.

3) Throw yourself into some other activity (no, not into someone else's arms, that isn't really a good idea because you will probably end up getting hurt twice over). Take up

LAUGHTER IS GOOD FOR YOU

an energetic sport, such as aerobics or line-dancing. Why not audition for a part in the next school or village production? Or anything to take your mind off a certain person.

4) Friends and family can be a great source of comfort, of course.

5) Don't beg the person to go out with you still or write him or her poems and letters, or give them little presents.

● The scene

Amy has succeeded in persuading Baz to take her to see the film *Romeo and Juliet*. This has not been a monumental success, as Baz fell asleep during the film and Amy had to wake him up when it was over. He then said he felt bad about it because he was already going out with Judy, who had also been asking him to take her to see *Romeo and Juliet*. Finally, he tells Amy that he cannot go out with her again.

Amy is deeply upset. Later that night, alone in her room, she writes a poem to Baz entitled 'Baz, wherefore art thou?'. She puts the poem in an envelope and posts it through Baz's letterbox first thing the following morning. Later that day she finds a letter pushed through her own letterbox. It is in Baz's handwriting. She opens it with trembling fingers. It reads as follows:

Dear Amy,

Please don't send me any more little poems because my mum read it and she started asking all sorts of questions. I really like you but not that much.

Cheers, Baz

As love-letters go, this letter scores minus several million, and Amy feels doubly hurt and rejected.

WHAT SHOULD AMY DO?

● Best thing to do: Arrange to see a really

funny film with Angelica, and have a good laugh. Leave Baz alone.

● **Another best thing to do:** Poems are usually an intensely personal expression of feelings which other people may find hard to understand or appreciate. Similarly, writing letters will probably make you feel better because what you have written makes perfect sense to you. But you will feel dreadful if you send the letter, and the person to whom you have sent it starts arguing with it, or says that they don't understand it, or – even worse – ignores it completely.

If you have something to say, it is better to say it to someone's face. If you can't imagine yourself doing that, then it is probably better to keep your distance, and refrain from poetry and from spilling all your deepest thoughts and feelings into a letter.

PROBLEM FIVE: Sibling rivalry or friend rivalry

● **The scene - 1**

Angelica and Amy both like the same boy, Scott. He is new to their school, and they are both keen to talk to him, show him around, sit next to him and be his 'friend'. In fact they would both like to be more than friends with him. There is a slight problem.

WHAT ANGELICA HOPES AMY WILL DO:

1) Find someone else to be interested in.
2) Develop an illness, not a serious one, but enough to keep her away from school for a while.
3) Break out in zits and cold sores.

WHAT AMY HOPES ANGELICA WILL DO:

1) Find someone else to be interested in.
2) Develop an illness, not a serious one, but enough to keep her away from school for a while.
3) Break out in zits and cold sores.

Neither of these things happen. So what *does* happen?

Angelica comes to school wearing a skirt which seems to have got shorter since the day before.

The following day Amy arrives at school in a skirt which is even shorter. They both walk as near to Scott as possible, and glare at each other's hemlines.

Angelica wears her favourite perfume to school, and sits next to Scott.

The next day Amy wears *her* favourite perfume (at least half a bottle of it), and sits on the other side of Scott. Halfway through geography, Scott asks if he can open a window because he feels in need of some fresh air.

At lunch-time Angelica offers Scott half a Kit-Kat. Amy

FRIEND RIVALRY

immediately offers him a whole Mars bar. Scott explains that he doesn't really like chocolate. They both offer him some of their crisps, and Amy is distraught when Scott chooses to share Angelica's salt and vinegar flavour in preference to her own cheese and onion pack.

This sort of thing continues for several days. Amy and Angelica argue over which of them is more attracted to Scott. They each write a poem to Scott (which they wouldn't dare show him). They show each other their poems, and they both declare each other's poem to be rubbish. They have a major falling-out, and stop speaking.

In the meantime, Scott has chosen to sit next to Arabella Proudfoot, and has asked her out. Arabella has been totally cool to Scott for weeks. She has hardly smiled at him and seemed very distant. (Remember everyone likes a challenge and making yourself too available can be a turn-off.)

So the whole thing has been a complete waste of time, and there was no point in falling out. A certain amount of damage has been done to their friendship, but Amy and Angelica decide to patch things up.

Remember that friends are more important than 'chasing rainbows' (or chasing Scott, or whoever it happens to be). Don't lose your friends along the way when you might trip and fall and never catch that elusive butterfly. (Poetic, or what?)

Don't argue or shout at your friend, especially when the person you both like is around. He or she will most certainly be put off coming near either of you.

Never say nasty or untrue things behind your friend's back. The person you are attracted to won't like you for it. They will like you a whole lot more if you are friendly and straightforward, rather than consumed with jealousy and hostility towards your rival.

● The scene - 2

William Warmwell has asked Angelica out for the evening. They are going to a film. Amy feels left out. "You were going to come round to my house," she complains to Angelica. "I thought we were going to dye our hair red again, and swap some clothes."

"There'll be other evenings," Angelica replies.

"I doubt it. You'll be out all the time with William Warm-and-Wonderful."

"Are you jealous?"

"No."

● **Question:** Is Amy jealous?

● **Answer:** Yes.

● What can Angelica do about this?

1) She can reserve some time to spend with Amy, doing the things they enjoy doing together. She can tell her that she values their friendship.

2) She could ask William if he has a friend who would like to make up a foursome with Amy, so that they can all go to the cinema together. This would probably be better than asking Amy to join them on her own, as she would inevitably feel that she was just tagging along and not really wanted.

● What can Amy do about this?

1) She can talk about her feelings openly with Angelica, and admit to feeling left out or jealous. If they are good friends, they should be able to discuss the situation and treat each other's feelings sympathetically.

2) She can try very hard to be pleased for Angelica, and realise that sooner or later her turn will come too, and someone will ask her out. When this happens, it will be equally important to have a good friend to talk to, when things are going well and when they aren't.

● What they both need to remember:

They are both growing and changing as individuals and so their friendship is evolving as well. A real friendship will encompass all the changes, get stronger, and stand the test of time.

PROBLEM SIX: Peer pressure

● The scene

Amy has not entirely given up on attracting Scott's attention. She tags along with the crowd he is in, and they all head for the recreation ground. Once they are there, Scott lights a cigarette. Amy is fervently anti-smoking, and hates everything about it. But suddenly she sees it as an opportunity to impress Scott, and be like him.

"Can I have one?" she asks.

"Sure. Here. Want a light?"

Amy puts the cigarette in her mouth. It wobbles because she is nervous, and it takes several attempts to light it. Then she inhales deeply. Everything turns black, and she feels sick.

"Are you OK? You've gone really pale."

"Er, yes, I'm fine."

Meanwhile, Scott has wandered off. He doesn't seem the least bit impressed that Amy is smoking.

● The moral of this: If you hate smoking,

or anything else for that matter, but feel you have to do it in order to impress someone, ask yourself if that person is really worth it. You will probably end up with all sorts of smoking-related diseases – and that person will long since have vanished from your life (gone up in a puff of smoke – ha ha).

ER, YES, I'M FINE!

Remember that trying to be like someone is no way to get them to like you. If you copy them all the time, you are more likely to end up annoying them.

You may feel that the people around you put pressure on you to dress or behave in a certain way (which you know isn't really you) in order to fit in. Have the courage to be different. Wear what suits you. Anyone who laughs at you isn't worth knowing. Sooner or later someone will be interested in *you*, not just the clothes you wear.

Most people can't afford to be the height of fashion the whole time, or to have all the things that advertisements and people who watch advertisements are always telling you you *must* have.

CHAPTER 3
School and Your Social Life

SO WHAT DOES YOUR SCHOOL REALLY DO FOR YOUR SOCIAL LIFE?

A lot depends on the head of the school, and how much emphasis they place on social activities. Hours and hours of maths, English, geography etc. have never been particularly conducive to a riotous social life. If you have heaps of homework, you may not have a lot of time left over for parties, discos, and so on. You will probably feel more like flopping into bed and giving your poor, overloaded brain a rest.

On the plus side, if there is someone at school who you like very much, it is nice to know you will be seeing them every day, and possibly even sitting next to them. You can join the group they are in to get closer to them, although this is not always without its own problems:

PROBLEM ONE: Finding things at school which are good for your social life

● The scene

Luke Loofah is a leading light in the St Herbert's Drama Group. Angelica thinks he is dreamy, and longs to get to know him. He is two years ahead of her, and she hardly ever gets to see him. So she decides to join the drama group, and take part in their next production, *The Wizard of Oz*, with a rap interpretation of the song, 'We're off to see the wizard/the wonderful wizard of Oz,' composed by Luke Loofah himself. Luke is to take the part of the Tin Man, for which he intends to wrap himself up in silver foil. Angelica offers to help him do this, Luke declines.

"Look, Angelica, I hate to tell you this but there isn't really anything left for you to do."

CHOOSE AN ACTIVITY WHICH SUITS YOUR PARTICULAR ABILITY

"But I can dance! Look!"
Luke looks unimpressed.

"And I can act!" Angelica rushes madly about the stage, shouting, "Where's the wizard? Where is he? I must find him!"

"Er, sorry . . ."

"Hey, Luke!" someone says. "If she's willing, we could use that lion costume."

Angelica shouts, "Oh, yes! Anything!"

And so she finds herself in the back end of a lion costume made for two people. Unsurprisingly, it is a non-speaking part, and it is hot and uncomfortable. Her back aches, and when she is finally allowed to get out of the costume and stand upright, her hair looks like a damp bird's nest, her face has gone bright red and there is perspiration dripping off her nose.

"Thanks, Angelica!" says Luke, passing by and giving her

GREAT STUFF, KID!

BAD SOCIAL MOVE:
TRYING TOO HARD TO IMPRESS

a slap on her aching back which nearly sends her flying off the stage. "You're a good sport!"

Angelica grins weakly.

In other words, choose an activity which suits your particular ability. Don't try to impress people by taking on more than you can handle. It won't work. You may have a captive audience at school, but once outside the school gates they'll run miles from you if you keep showing off.

THINGS THAT *ARE* GOOD FOR YOUR SOCIAL LIFE:

1) School orchestra/choir/art/drama/nature group (not 'naturist')/any kind of extra-curricular group or activity.

2) Sports (see chapter seven).

3) The school bus. You are obliged to get to know the idiots who keep stuffing things down the back of your shirt, singing loudly in your ear and asking to borrow your ruler, pencil, rubber etc. as they desperately attempt to draw a straight line in their maths homework book before the bus lurches round the next corner.

4) The school canteen. This may or may not be particularly good for your health, but at least you get to sit with your friends, and eating is meant to be a social activity (unless you eat like a pig, like Elspeth Hoggins or Kev Winterbotham).

GOOD SOCIAL MOVE:

EATING TOGETHER (UNLESS YOU ARE
ELSPETH HOGGINS OR KEVIN WINTERBOTHAM)

5) A small school. There don't seem to be many of these left, but if you are lucky enough to be part of a small school, you may enjoy the friendly atmosphere in which everyone knows everyone else, although sometimes this can be a little stifling.

6) A large school. There are plenty of these. It may take a while to find your feet (again), or even your way around. But with so many facilities and so many people, there must be something and someone for you somewhere. It is just a matter of time before you find them, or they find you.

7) Co-educational school. You would assume, naturally, that this must be good for your social life. It should also create a more relaxed atmosphere, in which boys and girls grow up together as friends. But beware of treating school as nothing more than a stepping-stone to a better social life.

For instance, when Mr Prenderghastly the maths master sets your maths homework, and tells you it has to be in by Friday, it will not go down too well if you immediately whip out your pocket social diary, and say: "Look, I can't do anything about it tonight because I'm going to the cinema with Colin. Now, tomorrow's Wednesday, isn't it? Hmmm . . . I'm going skateboarding with the guys straight after school, then it's Aquafun with my best mate at the leisure centre, I can't possibly miss that, and I've got a friend coming round later to discuss a party we're arranging. I'll need my beauty sleep after that lot! Which brings us to Thursday. Oh, wow! It's the concert! I've got tickets for a gig by a band called Jamsplat, they're really cool. I'll be dead tired the next day. I could probably fit the maths in at the weekend, if that's OK with you."

Is it OK with Mr Prenderghastly? No, it isn't. Mr Prenderghastly used to be a sergeant-major in the army before he became a maths teacher, and he is not impressed by your laid-back attitude to schoolwork, and deep commitment to enjoying yourself.

The worst thing that can happen if you don't bother with work is that you end up having to do even more work in order to catch up, retake exams, and so on. You may find yourself falling behind all your friends academically, and this may even affect you socially, as they all move onwards and upwards, and you stay exactly where you are, under the hawk-like eye and beak-like nose of Mr

Prenderghastly. Always remember that things like detentions are definitely NOT good for your social life.

8) Schools often organise end-of-term fun things like plays and parties – all good for letting your hair down (except that you cannot let it down because it is full of hair gel and hairspray).

PROBLEM TWO: How to overcome things at school that are not good for your social life

● The scene

Baz is trying to catch up on a lot of schoolwork he has not yet done, and he is also trying to catch up on a lot of sleep

CATCHING UP ON LOST SLEEP DURING
SCHOOL HOURS IS NOT A GOOD IDEA

he has not yet had, for various reasons (band practice, Steve's party, more band practice, Steve's next party, and so on). Unfortunately, he cannot catch up on his work and on his sleep at the same time. He arrives at school late again, bleary-eyed, and finds himself standing next to someone new to the school. Her name is Karen, and she is stunningly beautiful (even at nine a.m. and in school uniform – how does she do it?). Suddenly Baz wishes he had gone to bed earlier last night so that he wasn't so tired. He regrets his crumpled uniform, stuffed unceremoniously under the bed last night and thrown on in two minutes flat this morning when he was already late. He feels a little foolish because Mrs Broke has not yet found the time to let the turn-ups on his trousers down, so the trousers are too short. She has also ironed the creases in the wrong place. His trainers are covered in mud, and the laces are undone. Anyway, even if Karen wasn't put off by his appearance, Baz knows he has so much work to catch up on that he doesn't really have any time left for a social life. He feels depressed. In fact, there is a lot you can do to combat the major threats which school poses to your social life:

MAJOR THREAT NUMBER ONE – School uniform: Not many people are wildly attracted to a ghastly green/maroon/navy/grey, shapeless blob, which is what your school and the washing-machine together will attempt to turn you into. You can minimise the damage by acquiring clothes which are the right school colours but better made and more flattering than the standard issue school uniform. More and more schools are allowing you

to do this. Roll-necks and polo necks, for instance, are smart and (recently) fashionable. You can wear one under your school sweatshirt. (If you are a girl – obviously – you can hitch up your skirt one centimetre at a time so that gradually it becomes a miniskirt. You can blame this on the fact that you are *growing*.)

MAJOR THREAT NUMBER TWO –
Having to get up early: This is especially bad if you have to catch a bus or train, or even be ready in time for a lift. You may not be at your sparkling best first thing in the morning (it takes at least until midday for your brain to kick in and you do not usually get up at weekends until lunch-time which, as everyone knows, is at four p.m.). So it is a terrible shock to the system when the alarm goes off at six thirty a.m. and you go back to sleep till seven thirty and then have to rush madly, hair unbrushed, uniform flapping (you look like a mad bat out of hell if your uniform is black), to be at the bus-stop or station by seven forty-five a.m. You arrive at school looking pale and uninteresting, with mad hair and staring, bleary eyes. Only to realise (rather like Baz) that the most fantastic-looking girl/boy in the entire school (and universe) is standing right next to you, asking you the time.

"Er . . . I . . . er . . . I . . . er . . ." you gibber helplessly. And then he or she is gone, without waiting for an answer. Can you blame them? School can be cruel. What is the answer? Go to bed earlier. Simple.

EXCUSE ME – CAN YOU TELL ME THE TIME?

MAJOR THREAT TO SOCIAL LIFE:
HAVING TO GET UP EARLY

MAJOR THREAT NUMBER THREE –
Homework: You can sometimes turn this to your advantage by doing it in the company of a friend. Tell your parents you are working on a project together. You can also ask someone you really like to help you, either by lending you a pen, ruler or book, or by going through it with you. Tell them how clever you think they are. They will be flattered, although maybe a little taken aback if the subject you want their help with is not one they are particularly good at.

MAJOR THREAT NUMBER FOUR –
Single sex schools: You cannot really find an

environment less likely to help with a happy social life. Single sex schools do try to compensate by organising sporting fixtures or dances at other single sex (opposite sex) schools. It is probable that at these sporting fixtures no one can really keep their eye on the ball, or concentrate on what they're meant to be doing, so starved have they been of the company of the opposite sex. At the dances arranged for them, they either go completely mad or else stand around like petrified rabbits caught in the strobe lights.

WHAT'S THE SOLUTION?

You could set up a social club at the school and arrange as many parties, outings and so on, as possible.

CHAPTER 4
Your Family and Your Social Life

You may find that your idea of what your social life should be (the party scene, the club scene, fantastic boyfriend/girlfriend, fun! fun! fun! forget sleep . . . don't worry, Mum/Dad, I'll be back by four a.m.) may differ in some respects from your parents' idea of what your social life should be (ballroom dancing lessons and a general knowledge quiz night for all ages at your school organised by the Parent/Teacher Association – "Don't worry, dear. We'll be there to encourage you!").

Remember that it is a testing time for both you and your parents. It is a fairly new idea for them that you should have a social life of your own which does not involve them, and they will obviously be concerned about you. They may have become used to going out as a family or, at least, taking you to well-organised, supervised events and clubs (Guides, Scouts, St John's Ambulance, local choir, and so on). What they are not used to is seeing you go out as a teenager and it may be hard for them to stand at the door and wave as you disappear down the road.

Your parents must accept to a certain extent (as far as a normal parent is able, which is not *too* far, so don't push it!) the inevitability of your breaking away from the close-knit family unit in order to find your own feet (yes! I *know* they're at the end of your legs!), and your own circle of friends. You are beginning to reach out for independence and to search for your own place in society. This is a natural process to which most parents will give gentle encouragement – unless they wish you to be still living at home at the age of forty.

PROBLEM ONE: Making the break from the familiar routine too suddenly

● The scene

Amy has gone to her room to change out of her school uniform. Usually it takes about two minutes. Then she is ready to flop into her favourite armchair and watch Children's BBC. However, today she does not emerge from her room for nearly two hours except to disappear into the bathroom for a while. Eventually she comes downstairs and finds herself face to face with her father. Her hair has changed colour from mouse to haystack blonde and she has made it spiky with loads of hair gel. She has used very pale foundation on her face, strong, dark eye make-up and very loud lipstick. She is wearing a bright green top and long brown skirt and dangly green earrings . . . so she looks a bit like a tree.

"Wh . . . what happened?" stammers Mr Average.

"Er . . . perhaps I just grew up," says Amy.

This is NOT a good answer since the average parent does not necessarily equate your hair changing colour with growing up.

"And where do you think you are going, looking like

that?" enquires Mrs Average, appearing from the kitchen.

"Out," replies Amy.

"Out where?"

"Oh! Just out. You know . . ."

No. They don't know. They don't ever want to know.

PREDICTABLE PARENTAL REACTION TO TOO MANY SIGNS OF 'GROWING UP'

And they will most certainly NOT be letting Amy out of the house until she at least looks like the daughter they are used to.

So don't use shock tactics and expect your parents to be impressed if you suddenly look grown-up. They are more likely to be alarmed, and a worried parent is unlikely to let you out of the house. Remember: a worried parent is a difficult parent, a parent who is likely to say "No". It is much better to look reasonably normal: you can still make yourself look good without going completely over the top.

A WORRIED PARENT IS A **PROBLEM** PARENT, A PARENT WHO LIKES TO SAY 'NO'

If you really want to experiment with wild clothes, hair and make-up, it is probably better to do so at home in the company of a friend, and have a good laugh before you wash it all off again. Accustom your family gradually to seeing you experiment with your appearance; impress upon them that it is just a bit of fun. You may even accept some of their advice on what suits you and what does not. (OK! So you will never accept your father's opinion that you would look good in a kilt.)

In other words, tread carefully if you want your parents

to open the door and let you out into the world. This is especially important if they tend to be over-protective.

PROBLEM TWO: "Help! They won't let me out!"

If you are the oldest you might have more problems breaking away from home because your parents aren't used to the idea of their baby birds leaping out of the nest and flying away. They will need plenty of reassurance that you are still a homing pigeon and will be back in the nest at a certain time (make sure you are). If you're the youngest, the way is often paved by older siblings, and your parents will probably be more relaxed about the idea of letting you go out. Unless, of course, your older sibling has completely messed things up, in which case be prepared for comments like: "IF YOU THINK I'M LETTING YOU OUT OF THIS HOUSE AFTER WHAT YOUR SISTER DID, YOU'D BETTER THINK AGAIN!" If this happens to you, try to look and behave as unlike your sister as possible. If she wears loads of make-up and dresses like Josi, the wildest member of the Nut Girls, you should appear quiet and studious, wearing a long skirt, sensible shoes and no make-up at all. Tell your parents that you wish to join a serious discussion group. This is not far from the truth as you and your friends are always having serious discussions about boys, make-up, clothes and the Nut Girls.

With any luck your older sister or brother will have behaved themselves, and you will be able to walk into a ready-made social life and mix with all their friends and their friends' younger siblings. This is not always the case if, like Angelica, you have an older sibling, like Grant, who never goes anywhere. Or you may have fiercely over-protective parents (remember they are only like that because they care).

● The scene
Soumik Sen would like to go out skateboarding with some friends who have just knocked at the door. Mr and Mrs Sen have never met these friends before and they tend to be very suspicious of people they have never met . . . and of the world in general outside the family home. They are worried about Soumik getting mixed up with people who are a bad influence and might get their son involved with drugs.

● What Soumik hopes his parents will say: "Yes, Soumik. You can go out with your friends. We will see you later."

● What Mr and Mrs Sen actually say: "No, it is not the right time to go skateboarding. You must get on with your homework."

● What can Soumik do about this?: He can prepare his parents by bringing a friend he knows they'll love to his house, to break them in gently. Hopefully they will feel reassured that Soumik's friends are perfectly 'normal', bright and cheerful individuals. Then

Hair – not too much of it. Gleams with health.

Honest, open expression Disarming smile.

Looks (and dresses) just like his father (Your parents like his father)

Smart shoes (well-polished)

THE SORT OF FRIEND YOUR PARENTS WOULD APPROVE OF

Mr and Mrs Sen will feel happier about letting Soumik go off on his skateboard as long as he has all the right protective gear and he promises to be back by a certain time.

PROBLEM THREE: "Help! They won't let me stay in!"

● The scene – 1

Grant Toogood's parents are worried that their son does not go out enough. They worry that he is lonely and isolated because all he does is watch television and read books. He has tried explaining to them that he is perfectly happy on his own but they don't believe him. So they scour the local newspaper for all kinds of social events which they insist he goes to. In the last week he has been to a pottery class, on a thirty kilometre hike with the Young Ramblers' Association, to a dance organised by the Young Conservatives, another dance organised by the Young Farmers, to a Scottish Dancing class, a floodlit evening picnic organised by the Young Local History Association, a lecture on the secret life of the hedgehog followed by wine, cheese, bread and saucers of milk, and choir practice. Grant's sister, Angelica, has had to go to most of these events with him. Now both Grant and Angelica are utterly exhausted and wish Mr and Mrs Toogood would let them stay in and watch TV.

● How do you deal with this?: You
can avoid being endlessly organised by 'getting a life' of your own. Perhaps your parents really would like a little time on their own as well as wanting you to go out and enjoy yourself.

● Best strategy: Bear in mind that if you have
already decided before you go to the next meeting of the local amateur dramatic society that it is going to be BORING/DEADLY DULL/EMBARRASSING then you are most unlikely to get anything out of it. However, if you let your guard down just a little bit you might begin to be aware of a strange new sensation (enjoying yourself). And if you open up just a little bit to someone (ask them their name, how long have they been acting/playing volleyball, what they like to watch on TV, what music they like, and so on) you might begin to make a friend. Once you find a friend of your own and an activity you enjoy you can begin to organise your own life, and your parents will feel less need to organise your life for you.

● The scene - 2
Soumik is still having a hard time. In order to retain control of their son's social life, and to protect him from the dangerous influence of strangers, Mr and Mrs Sen try to arrange suitable friends for him. They want to make sure he is with people of whom they approve. So they invite their friends who happen to have a daughter of the 'right' age for Soumik to meet. The girl, who looks as though she would like the floor to open up and swallow her, sits

between her parents on one sofa, and Soumik finds himself sandwiched between Mr and Mrs Sen on another sofa. The parents beam at one another and pass round plates of food.

"Well," says Mrs Sen brightly, "Soumik and Aneena seem to be getting on well."

How on earth can she say that? Soumik wonders, considering that he and Aneena have not exchanged a single word. So what can he do?

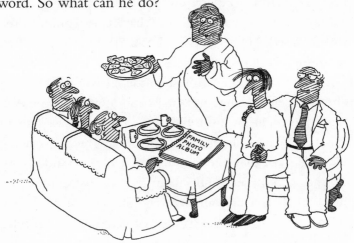

● **The wrong thing** to do at this stage, however tempting it may be, is to say something like, "Hey, you guys, I've got to go – Baz has got a new snakeboard and he wants me to time him. See you!" Escaping like this through the door and running (or skateboarding) as fast and as far as possible from a difficult social situation may make your life easier for a short while. Unfortunately the same problem will be there when you return home. All Mr and Mrs Sen's suspicions will have been confirmed, and their efforts to control their son's life will be redoubled.

● **A better solution** by far is to take control of the situation yourself. This may cause a few raised eyebrows, but it may impress upon your parents that you have a mind of your own without actually causing offence. Soumik could say something like, "Come on, Aneena, I've got a pretty cool computer game which you may like to have a go at. And may I get Aneena and me another drink of Coke, Mum? It's this way to the kitchen, Aneena."

Aneena may not turn out to be the love of Soumik's life, the girl he wishes to marry, or anything like that, but she is probably feeling as awkward and embarrassed as he is, and he can at least be friendly towards her. She might even become a friend.

Later on, Soumik could try having a gentle chat with his parents about how difficult he finds it to make friends unless he is allowed to do so on his own, without his parents present. He could thank them for their efforts on his behalf and maybe suggest that he and Aneena be allowed to go together to some social event or sports or other kind of club.

PROBLEM FOUR: Embarrassing questions

● **The scene**

Baz has been to a party. It wasn't a particularly great party, and now he has a headache and just wants to go to sleep. However, Mrs Broke is full of questions, starting with the most difficult one: "How was it?" Perhaps realising how impossible it is to answer this question except with the words "OK, I suppose" or "Fine" or "So-so" (which tells the person asking the question absolutely nothing) she launches straight into a flurry of annoying little questions: "Who was there? What did you do? Did you dance? Did you meet anyone nice, dear? What did you have to eat/drink?" Baz stares at his mother blankly. His brain has already retired for the night.

How do you deal with the awkward questions? They are as inevitable as night follows day.

DON'T stare blankly at the parent asking the questions. They will only start worrying that your mind has fallen under some bad influence.

DON'T ignore them completely and rush upstairs to your room: they will suspect you have something to hide.

Instead, prepare your answers in advance as follows:

● **Question:** "Who was there?"

● **Bad answer:** "Oh, loads of people, I don't know." The vagueness of this answer will conjure up in the parental mind visions of some wild and totally unsupervised rave.

● **Good answer:** Mention a few names familiar to your parents of people they know and like. Mention an adult who was present. They will feel reassured to know that the party was properly organised and supervised.

● **Question:** "What did you do?"

OH, LOADS OF
PEOPLE ... I DON'T
KNOW ...

VAGUE ANSWERS GIVE RISE TO PARENTAL
ANXIETY

● **Bad answer:** "Dunno, really. I can't remember." Your parent will not be at all happy to be told that you can't remember what has happened to you during the last few hours. You must reassure them that your mind is still functioning as it should.

● **Good answer:** "I talked to people. I sat on the stairs for a while and talked to Mark. I played a computer game. I took my trainers off because my feet were killing me. After that, people seemed to avoid me for some reason." The more mundane details you can fill in, the more reassured your parent will feel. They can visualise you at the party, just being yourself and not behaving too

WHERE DID EVERYONE GO?

BAD SOCIAL MOVE:

TAKING YOUR TRAINERS OFF

wildly or out of character, which is what they are worried about.

● Question:

"Did you dance?" You may find that every time you go to a party your parent (especially your mother) develops a strange preoccupation with whether or not you danced, as if this fact held some kind of special significance.

● Bad answer: "No." If you are a girl your mother will start worrying that you are a shy wallflower, and that she or someone else is going to have to do something to bring you out. She won't leave you alone and there will be endless questions along the lines of, "Is something upsetting you, dear? Is there anything you want to talk about?" You will end up wondering if there really *is* something wrong with you because you did not dance. And if you are a boy you may find yourself frogmarched off to toe-curlingly embarrassing dancing lessons, God forbid!

● Good answer: "Yes." This answer will bring a smile to your mother's face. It is not really worth trying to explain that it was a party at which no one danced and

you would have felt stupid dancing on your own. So why not say "Yes" and leave it at that?

TOE-CURLINGLY EMBARRASSING 'DANCING LESSONS'

● **Question:** "Did you meet anyone nice, dear?"

● **Bad answer:** "No. They were all horrible." It is not a good idea to be flippant, especially late at night when you and your parents are all tired. It will not go down well. Even if you really do feel that all the people at the party were horrible, it is most unlikely to be true. You were almost certainly unlucky or talking to the wrong people.

Perhaps you are on the defensive. You really *did* meet someone nice, but you would rather not discuss it with your parents. However, there is no need to put them off the trail with quite such a cutting answer. Go for a quieter, parent-pacifying remark such as, "Yes, there were lots of nice people." A truly persistent parent will then fix you with a look and say, "Anyone in particular?" At this stage you don't know why but you cannot seem to help yourself: you find yourself looking as stupid as you feel, blushing bright red, drawing a circle on the carpet with your big toe and not knowing quite what to do with your hands. You try desperately to avoid catching your parent's eye. WHY DO PARENTS DO THIS TO YOU? Now there is a truly unanswerable question! So, after this, it should come as quite a relief to move on to the next question, which is rather more straightforward:

● **Question:** "What did you have to eat/drink?"

● **Bad answer:** "Fourteen glasses of wine and a sausage roll." This answer will almost certainly guarantee that you are never EVER allowed out to a party again. Under-age drinking is a *big* problem, posing a major threat to health and personal safety, and your parents have to be sure you are safe.

● **Good answer:** "Fourteen sausage rolls and three cans of Coke. Amy's dad let me try some of the party punch, and then we had pizza." Parents are always impressed, and occasionally bankrupted, by the teenage appetite; they will also be reassured to know that there was an adult supervising the drinks.

There is one more question which you would be wise to avoid ever having to answer:

"WHAT TIME DO YOU CALL THIS?"

There is no good answer to this question, and you can avoid having to answer it at all by making sure that you are home when you said you would be. Don't be late. If you have been held up for some reason make sure you phone home to explain, or ask them to come and get you. Don't ever leave your parents wondering what on earth has happened to you. You may even find them phoning the police and the local hospitals or driving around the area looking for you – and although they will be relieved to see you they will also be VERY angry, and with good reason. Being grounded by your parents will not have a very good effect on your social life.

PROBLEM FIVE: When siblings sabotage your social life

● The scene

Mr and Mrs Toogood have gone out for the evening, leaving Grant to keep a 'Big Brother Is Watching You' eye on Angelica and Becky. Angelica phones Steve and asks him if he'd like to come round and watch a video (*Revenge of the Strangler Beans* – an offshoot of the *Killer Tomatoes* movie). "Yeah, sure," says Steve. "Mind if I bring James? I'm supposed to look after him – it's a real drag. Oh, and

Dave and Baz and Wazza are here – mind if they come too?"

Angelica says yes. Grant's only comment is, "Mum and Dad will go mad if they find out."

The evening is a riot. The film reduces everyone to fits of helpless mirth, after which there is a stampede into the kitchen to raid the fridge of its entire contents, including a leftover lasagne, a large piece of Brie, a salami sausage, Mr Toogood's cold beer and some of his wine. Then Steve and his friends leave.

Mr and Mrs Toogood return a little while later. Mrs Toogood goes to the fridge to get the milk for the bedtime drinks. "Where's everything gone?" she cries.

"What are these?" shouts Mr Toogood, picking up Steve's 'cool shades', which he has left behind in Mr Toogood's favourite armchair.

⬤ **What Angelica is hoping her brother and sister will say:** NOTHING.

⬤ **What Grant actually says:** "I think you had better sort this one out with Angelica." (Thanks, Grant.)

⬤ **What Becky says:** "Steve came round with his brother. James is really nice, you know. He's asked me out tomorrow night. But Steve drank your wine." (THANKS FOR NOTHING, BECKY. I'LL KILL YOU LATER.)

I THINK YOU'D BETTER
SORT THIS ONE OUT WITH
ANGELICA

STEVE WAS HERE — AND JAMES !

THIS IS KNOWN AS 'DROPPING YOU IN IT'

⬤ **How to avoid this sort of situation:** It is definitely a bad idea to tell lies to your parents. It is an even worse idea to expect your siblings to lie to your parents on your behalf. Sooner or later someone will say the wrong thing and the truth will come out. You will be covered in confusion, shame and embarrassment.

It is not worth it.

If you want your siblings to be on your side don't ask them to do or say things that are likely to land them in trouble. Instead why not turn the relationship to your advantage? There are a number of ways in which you can do this.

WAYS IN WHICH SIBLINGS CAN BE GOOD FOR YOUR SOCIAL LIFE:

1) Baby-sitting. If you have to baby-sit for younger brothers or sisters (or even for friends' younger brothers and sisters) make sure you baby-sit responsibly. If you show yourself to be a good baby-sitter you will be asked to baby-sit again. Suggest that you should be paid 'the going rate' for this. Most people are happy to reward someone who is helpful and responsible. You can then put the money you earn towards a new improved social life (a visit to the cinema or an extra portion of French fries at McDonald's depending on how generous the person paying you is).

2) Younger sister or older brother's friends. You may think your little sister is a complete pain or that your older brother is an idiot with stupid hair and an annoying laugh. But think again . . . one day your brother or sister may walk in with a most spectacularly beautiful friend.

3) You can borrow their clothes, their make-up, their shower gel etc. It is probably a good idea to ask first. If you stay on good terms with them they are more likely to lend you their support when you need it. You may even become quite close, it can be very comforting to have a sister to confide in or a big brother to put his arm round you occasionally.

4) If you and your siblings think your parents are being totally unreasonable about something, you can plan your strategies together. You may have to arrive at some sort of compromise with your parents.

PROBLEM SIX: Organising your social life from home

HERE'S WHAT YOU NEED:

1) A telephone.

2) A complete absence of parents or annoying siblings while you make your call.

The first requirement is easier to organise than the second. If it is totally impossible to find a quiet moment or a quiet corner in which to make your call (or perhaps you don't have a telephone), you may prefer to use a phonebox. This is not such an attractive idea if it is pouring with rain, the temperature is well below freezing, you have no loose change and it is a kilometre to the nearest phonebox. Using a phonebox is also a risky business since you may run out of change just at a critical moment when the person on the other end (who you like a lot) was about to say something:

"You know, you're really . . ." (the phone goes dead, followed by a high-pitched whine). Really what? You search wildly in your pockets for loose change but it is TOO LATE. You will NEVER KNOW what the other person was about to say. ("You're really great,"? "You're really amazing,"? "You're really . . . weird,"?)

The same sort of thing can happen at home. Your parents come along at a critical moment during the phone call, when you're in the middle of organising a date, and say something like, "I think you've been on the phone long enough," or "Who are you talking to? Tell them you've got to go and have your supper. It's going cold." They make these remarks loudly and then they hover in the background, making it impossible for you to continue the conversation in a normal manner. You find yourself talking in a strangely stiff and unnatural tone of voice and the conversation, which had been going swingingly, ends abruptly: "Er. Well. I've got to go now. See you. Bye." When you've put the receiver down you realise you've forgotten to arrange a time to meet the love of your life, and it is all your parent's fault.

HOW DO YOU AVOID THIS SORT OF SITUATION?

Always ask if you can use the phone. If you show a little respect for your parents (and their phone bill), it is more likely that they will let you loose on the phone. Keep your calls reasonably short (less than two hours is probably a good guide, or less than five minutes if you know your parent is struggling to pay the bills).

CHAPTER 5
Parties

There are many different kinds of party, including your own party, someone else's party, a parental party, an older sibling's party, a Christmas party, a Hallowe'en party, a fancy dress party, a bonfire party, a house-warming party, a wedding party, a close or distant relation's party, an end-of-term party, a congratulations-you-have-finally-stopped-biting-your-fingernails party and, well, the list is endless. You don't really need a reason to have a party, but people usually manage to think of one. Your birthday is right at the top of the list.

GREAT MUSIC...
GREAT FOOD...
GREAT ATMOSPHERE...

LET'S PARTY !

The idea of a party is usually an attractive one. You immediately start thinking, Ah, yes! Loads of fun, loads of friends, loads of food, cool music, coloured lights in a darkened room in which to get close to the one you love, perchance to dance.

However, the reality seldom matches up to the expectation raised by the prospect of a party. Of course, some parties are better than others. Some people are better than others at giving parties. You may feel that you are more suited to going to parties than you are to giving them. But what if no one invites you? Problems, problems.

PROBLEM ONE: Organising a party for the first time (or how to have a party if you don't know anyone)

● The scene

Amy and Angelica are planning to throw a party for all the people they know. So far they have four people on their list: Soumik, Baz, and Steve and James Cash. Amy feels too embarrassed to ask them, and is trying to persuade Angelica to hand out the invitations, which the girls have designed themselves, made of pink card in the shape of hearts. It is to be a Valentine's party (it is now July, but they have kept postponing their party plans since February while they plucked up the courage to actually go ahead with it).

"Why don't we leave it for another month?"

"NO."

"Well, I'm not asking them."

"So I suppose I'll have to, then. Anyway, the whole thing's stupid."

"Why?"

"Because you can't have a party with just two girls and four boys."

"It'd be fun for us!"

"No it wouldn't. They'd all go off and talk about football and stuff, and we'd be left standing there like two great prunes."

"Well, thanks for that."

"Look, I'm just facing up to reality."

"That must be a shock for you."

The two girls fall into gloomy silence, and refuse to speak to one another for the next ten minutes.

"The problem is," says Angelica at last, "we need more people."

"Can I help?" asks Angelica's little sister, Becky, poking her head round the door. She has been standing outside listening, as usual. "If I come to your party, then there'll be three girls. I really like Baz, you know."

"THE ANSWER IS NO, BECKY, GO AWAY." Becky slinks away.

So, if you won't invite little brothers and sisters to your party, what are your other options? Presumably you don't really want to invite your parents, although it is highly likely that one or both of them will insist on being present, or at least nearby, wherever you choose to hold the party. Many parents prefer to hire a school or village hall for the evening rather than have a teenage disco party in their own homes. Goodness knows why!

⬤ **Angelica has a bright idea:** "We could just invite the whole class."

"Apart from Elspeth Hoggins. She's just too awful."

You will have to decide for yourself whether inviting the whole of your class or year at school is a bright idea or not. It is really very unkind to leave just one or two people out because you don't happen to like them. On the other hand, you may end up with rather too many people to cater for.

⬤ **Bright idea two:** "I know, why don't we invite Emma Puddlestrop?"

"But she's AWFUL! And she's only twelve."

"I *know*. But she has a fantastic brother. You know, Pete. He's in the year above us. He'd have to come with Emma, to look after her sort of thing. Because she's only twelve."

"Hmmm . . . it might work."

So – inviting people to bring their brothers and sisters is not a bad idea (it's even quite a bright one).

⬤ **Bright idea three:** "Why don't we invite Mrs Merryweather? (Mrs Merryweather is a neighbour.)

"WHAAAT??! You cannot be serious!"

"I am. She's loads of fun. And besides, she has four sons. You know, Henry and Matthew are at our school, and the other two have just left, but we could ask her to bring them."

"I'm not sure about this . . ."

You could also ask your parents if they have friends or know of people with teenage offspring who you could invite. Your parents may have lost touch with old friends, and this is a good reason for contacting them again.

● **Not such a bright idea:** "Why don't we go for a walk round the town/village, and just invite everyone we meet?"

This is actually a recipe for disaster, because you are likely to end up with all sorts of gatecrashers and undesirables (ask your parent to explain what an undesirable is), and the party will not really be yours any longer. It will be out of control and there may even be trouble.

PROBLEM TWO: Surviving the party

● **The scene**
The disco lights are flashing, the darkened interior of the village hall is festooned with balloons and pink cardboard hearts (everywhere), and there is a table laden with party food and cans of Coke and an enormous pink Valentine heart-shaped cake made by Mrs Toogood. Mr Toogood, wearing a bow-tie, is presiding over the party punch. Angelica stands as far away as possible from her father and glares at him through the darkness. How could he come to her party wearing that naff bow-tie? She has decided to pretend that he is not her father but some barman she has hired for the evening. Her brother Grant is in charge of the

disco, which they have borrowed from the Cash family. He seems to be having a certain amount of trouble and every so often the music suddenly goes hyper and it sounds like the chipmunks are singing.

On top of all this, the party is going about as well as a wet weekend. As Angelica had anticipated, Soumik, Baz, Steve and James are all joking and laughing together, discussing football and their next gig, and ignoring everyone else. Angelica, Amy and Emma Puddlestrop are standing around like spare parts. Emma's dishy brother Pete brought her to the party, left her and went away again. So much for that bright idea.

Some more guests arrive, including Mrs Merryweather and her son Matthew (the other three sons haven't turned up). However, Matthew is actually quite good-looking . . . and suddenly, it is Mrs Merryweather to the rescue . . .

"Right, everyone!" she shouts, clapping her hands. "May I have your attention for a moment? Turn the music down, Grant, there's a good chap. No, I said down, not up. That's better."

"Oh my God!" Angelica whispers to Amy. "It's like we're at school. Oh, this is really embarrassing. This is really bad."

"I told you I wasn't sure about inviting her."

"OK, everyone!" continues Mrs Merryweather, totally unfazed. "Let's have a dancing competition! Mr Toogood and I will be the judges, but we'll be dancing too! Come on, everyone! Go for it! Now! Pump up the volume, Grant! Isn't that what they say?"

Anyway, there is no arguing with Mrs Merryweather, and soon everyone is dancing, and Angelica finds herself dancing with Matthew, which is great. He turns out to be a cool disco-dancing dude, and the party really begins to go with a swing.

And what's the moral of this tale? Simply that sometimes it is necessary to have someone (quite often an adult although it could be an older brother or sister) who will take charge of the party and organise some activity which will get everyone joining in. This is known as breaking the ice. Another way of breaking the ice is to give your party a theme, such as 'wear a hat'. Then you can all laugh at or admire each other's hats, swap hats, throw hats around, play hide-the-hat, and so on.

BEWARE FANCY DRESS PARTIES

But beware fancy dress parties. Sometimes they work. But the chances are that a lot of your friends won't bother to dress up, and you will feel a complete fool as a fairy-godmother, complete with wand, tiara and wide-spreading lacy skirts which you and everyone else keep tripping over. A lot of costumes are incredibly hot, and after several hours of energetic disco-dancing dressed as a brown bear in your mother's fake-fur coat, hat and boots, you will probably be rushed to hospital suffering from heat exhaustion, which is not a good end to any party. (You would have taken off the bear costume but you were only wearing your underwear underneath it, and it was not that sort of party.)

PROBLEM THREE: Going to a party when you don't know anyone

● The scene

Baz has been invited to a party in London by one of Steve's mates, who he doesn't know very well. Baz and Steve are staying with Steve's uncle and aunt at their flat. At the last minute Steve feels unwell and decides not to go to the party, so Baz goes on his own. There are a lot of people at the party, all talking and laughing and dancing with each other. Baz feels hot and uncomfortable, and wishes there was someone he could talk to. What should he do?

1) Leave. This is a solution, of course, but it is a hasty one, which may leave you wondering what might have happened if you had stayed a little longer. Parties sometimes improve, if you give them a chance.

2) Stand around looking mysterious and enigmatic (possibly wearing dark glasses). If you adopt this tactic, you look pretty cool to begin with, but you end up feeling very, very bored. Your cool and aloof exterior hopefully masks the fact that you are feeling uncomfortable and unsure of what to say or do, but it just ends up making matters worse, because no one feels encouraged to approach you.

MYSTERIOUS AND ENIGMATIC

VERY, VERY BORED

3) Find the kitchen. This is a much better, more practical solution. People who are feeling uncomfortable at parties generally migrate to the kitchen. There you'll find drink, food and quite possibly, a friend. Once you've made friends in the kitchen, you can go back to the party and, hopefully, enjoy it. Often *everybody* ends up in the kitchen. As kitchens tend to be quite small, you will find it easier to make contact with people as you'll be squashed up to them, and you can say "Excuse me" and "I can't breathe" and other interesting comments that might stimulate conversation.

4) Find the person who is giving the party and explain to them that you don't know anyone. If they are a good host, they should introduce you to some of their friends, or at least show you around.

5) There is usually *someone* at the party who is feeling as left out and awkward as you are. Find this person. You will recognise them because they look a bit like you (standing alone, looking mysterious and enigmatic). Ask them, "Do you know anyone at this party?" If the answer is "No", you immediately have something in common. (Except that it is no longer true because you now know each other!)

PROBLEM FOUR: A parental party

● The scene

Mr and Mrs Sen are giving a party in their home to celebrate the return of Mr Sen's brother from five years spent working in the north of England. He has now moved with his family into the same street as Mr and Mrs Sen. They have invited their neighbours, Mr Sen's colleagues from work, and most of their relations. The living-room is full of people, some standing, some sitting, all being incredibly polite to one another, even though they can hardly move. Some small cousins of Soumik's occasionally push through the forest of grown-up legs, momentarily knocking their parents off balance. A few drinks get spilled as a result, and there are profuse apologies as Mr Sen rushes to get the 1001 carpet-cleaner spray-gun and a J-cloth. Then it is back to the kitchen to fetch more plates of food and trays of drinks. Mr Sen is in charge of drinks, and Soumik is told to pass round the party nibbles.

THE WORST THINGS ABOUT PARENTAL PARTIES:

1) You are expected to take coats, hand round food, and so on. For this purpose, you are expected to look smart. You get all dressed up in your smartest, most sensible clothes,

and it doesn't really feel like you any longer. But you are much admired. You are obliged to wear a silly grin. If you look as bored and fed up as you feel, you will be in trouble and stand accused of spoiling your parents' evening.

2) Even if you are not expected to help, you may be invited down from your room to make a special guest appearance at your parents' dinner party. This is usually awful, as everyone turns to stare at you, as if you are some prize specimen. It is possible that the adults have run out of things to talk about, so you are wheeled in as a kind of conversation piece. They ask as many stupid questions as they possibly can, occasionally as though you are not even

in the room: "Good heavens, Marjorie, hasn't she shot up? How tall is she now?" When they have run out of questions, your parent will tell you they think you really ought to be getting back to your room, and haven't you got some homework to finish? (As if it was your idea in the first place to come down and interrupt their dinner party.) As you return to your room, you are aware that they are still talking about you, in somewhat hushed voices, and God only knows what they are saying.

HOW TO MAKE THE BEST OF THE WORST:

1) You could take refuge at a friend's house for the evening, if not for the whole night. Your parents might prefer to have you out of the way (cold-hearted lot that they are). And you have no desire to be in the way.

2) Or if it is a question of using you as a pair of hands (and legs) to pass round food etc., how about turning the whole thing into a business proposition? Say you'll throw in some washing-up as well if they'll pay you the going rate. Mention some entirely sensible thing that you are saving up for (a new schoolbag, for instance). They are not to know that you are actually saving up for the latest CD by Dr Drear and the Deadheads, including a free giant 3D poster of Dr Drear himself wearing only a pair of tartan boxer shorts.

3) If there is a sporting or other charity event for which you are being sponsored, NOW is the ideal moment to corner every adult in the room and get them to sign their name on your sponsorship form. If your parent raises an objection, simply turn round and tell them, "But it's for charity."

Of course, parental parties are not all as bad as the ones mentioned above. Sometimes they go to the other extreme, and completely let their hair down (not that many of them have much hair left, apart from the ageing hippy type, and often they are bald on top, just long and ponytailed at the back, and some are beginning to go grey). They have a few glasses of wine and start giggling. They

THINGS CAN GET VERY EMBARRASSING WHEN
YOUR PARENTS DECIDE TO 'DANCE'

call out embarrassing things to you, like, "How's your love life, then?" and then they *dance*. They put Phil Collins or someone on the stereo, kick off their shoes, and groove. This can be terribly embarrassing, or it can be quite funny, depending on your attitude. If you find it all horribly embarrassing you can either hide in your room or at a friend's house. Or if you find it quite funny, you may decide that if you can't beat them, why not join them? In extreme cases you may find yourself joining in a spot of line-dancing, or dancing a conga down the street, but don't worry about it. The comment you are most likely to pick up from your friends is, "Aren't your parents *fun*? I wish mine were." This kind of parent will almost certainly ask their friends to bring their offspring to the party, so there will be company for you, too. You can have your own little party in your room, or the kitchen, and everyone will be friendly, young and old alike.

This is not so likely to be the case at an older sibling's party.

PROBLEM FIVE: PNG at a party

First of all, what does this mean? PNG stands for *persona non grata*, which is Latin for 'person not wanted', which is basically what you are almost bound to be when your older brother or sister throws a party. You may be lucky, of course, and have an absolutely fabulous big sister or big brother who includes you in everything and finds your company an endless delight. (Do you come from a different planet?) But it is more usual to find yourself excluded.

● The scene

Steve is giving a party to which his younger brother James is NOT invited.

● What Steve says to James: "GET LOST!"

● What Mr and Mrs Cash say: "JAMES IS STAYING!"

Parents have an annoying habit of frustrating your efforts to get younger siblings out of the way. They are inclined to say things like: "You can't just push your little brother/sister out of the way for your own convenience," (Why not? What is the point in being an older sibling if you can't do this occasionally?), or "I'm not having your little brother/sister leave the house with their nasty sore throat." (Over-indulged little brat – your parents seem intent on turning them into a complete hypochondriac.)

If you are a younger sibling, of course, all of this can work in your favour.

It is much worse to be excluded from a party held by people of your own age, to which all your friends are invited.

HOW DO YOU DEAL WITH THIS?

1) Keep yourself busy on that particular day/evening. Arrange to go to see a film you've been wanting to see for

ages with someone. Also realise that there are almost bound to be a few other people who have not been invited, either. You could phone one of them and invite them over.

2) The following day, when everyone is feeling tired from last night's party, you will be refreshed by a good night's beauty sleep, and will particularly enjoy hearing comments like: "The party wasn't that great", or most likely, "I wish you'd been there, I didn't know you weren't invited."

3) Finally, consider that the people giving the party are not real friends if they don't include you. You can do without them.

PROBLEM SIX: Little brother or sister's party. How to survive it

● The scene

It is Baz's little half-sister Theodora's birthday. The house is full of balloons and the children have already burst quite a few of them. There are only four children in the house so far, but it seems like more. They are wildly excited, and running from room to room. Baz feels a headache coming on. His snakeboard is calling to him.

● **Question:** Should he leap on it and sail away into the distance?

LITTLE SIBLINGS' PARTY

● **Answer:** Yes, definitely. It is no good hiding in your room. They will seek you out. They will climb all over you, pull your hair, pull your earrings, tweak your nose, use you as a trampoline, turn your room upside-down, hide under your bed and grab you round the ankles, try out your deodorant and everything else they can lay their hands on, pull faces in your mirror, write rude messages on the glass in lipstick, and spill Coke and cheesy Wotsits all over your carpet and duvet. Unless you are the sort of person who enjoys this sort of thing and is seriously considering a career in child care, you had better get out now, before the little guests arrive, looking sweet and angelic in their party clothes (how deceptive appearances can be).

•CHAPTER 6
The Disco Scene

DO YOU SEE YOURSELF AS:

a) A disco-dancing dream?
b) A cool dancing dude?
c) A disco dork?
d) A disco duck?

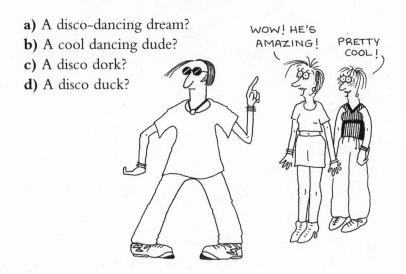

A COOL DANCING DUDE

AND DOES IT REALLY MATTER?

We have already observed that many mothers develop a strange preoccupation with their teenage darlings being able to trip the light fantastic round the dance floor, and "Did you dance, dear?" is a question you will almost certainly be asked at some stage.

If you are an Arabella Proudfoot who has been having ballet lessons since the age of three and has just won an award for advanced tap-dancing and a leading part in the

118

The Disco Scene

A DISCO DREAM

school production of *Riverdance*, there is obviously no problem. You only have to step on to the dance floor in your silver leotard and leggings, and everyone gasps and steps back in amazement to marvel as you dance like no one has ever danced before.

On the other hand, you may be a Kevin Winterbotham, who has trouble standing on one leg. Or, at least, standing first on one leg, and then the other, and then the other, and so on, as much in time to the music as is possible without falling over. Kevin's arms also become twice as long as they usually are when he is inside a disco, and they swing around wildly in all directions, knocking people flying. He seems to have very little control over them.

The chances are that you fall (maybe literally) somewhere between the two examples given above.

DISCO DORK

Everyone can dance, can't they? But you may lack confidence.

PROBLEM ONE: What to do if you can't/don't want to dance

● **Bad solution:** Well, you don't *have* to dance. It is not obligatory. However if, like Grant Toogood, you keep refusing when people take hold of your arm and try to get you to join in, they may begin to interpret your unwillingness as unfriendliness, or stand-offishness. If you insist too much that you hate dancing and that it's stupid, you are effectively calling all the other people at the disco stupid, and this will not make you very popular.

● **Better solution:** It is probably better to accept the well-meant invitations to join in. It is not actually how well you dance that matters. It is the fact that you join in with everyone else and enjoy yourself (go on – try) that really matters. If all you can manage, like Grant, is to close your eyes and sway slightly in time to the music, that's fine. People may worry to begin with that there is something wrong with you, and that you are about to pass out. But after a while they will conclude that you have a style all of your own, and that you are deeply into the music. That's the great thing about discos. You don't *have* to learn any particular steps, you can just do your own thing (whatever that is). Also, even if you really are an appalling dancer, most people are so worried about being appalling dancers themselves, they won't even notice you.

PROBLEM TWO: What to do if no one wants to dance with you

● **The scene**

Angelica has spent hours getting ready for the school disco (especially for people in her year and the year above). She has put on her whitest foundation and darkest eye make-up, dyed her hair deep red and put glitter in it, and put on a white stretch lace top and fluorescent orange leggings (great for dancing in). She and Amy have been practising some steps.

Once inside the school disco, they let rip. They give it their all. Angelica is aware that the boy she fancies is watching her, so she dances extra-energetically to further impress him. When she looks in his direction again, she is surprised to see that he has fled to a far corner of the school hall, where he is talking to a shy, mousy girl with glasses. And now he has asked the shy, mousy one to dance! Angelica is mortified. Why is this happening?

Why indeed.

⬤ **Answer:** Like Angelica, you may pride yourself on being able to dance spectacularly, but remember that other people may be intimidated by your fantastic performance. They may feel they can't get near you because your arms and legs are permanently flying in all directions. They probably feel they can't dance as well as you, and that you will laugh at them if they try.

The boy who Angelica likes may also be put off by her appearance. There is something quite challenging about the stark white make-up and contrasting dark eyes. He may feel safer with someone who looks more normal.

In other words, Angelica is trying too hard to impress, and it turns into overkill, and puts the person she wishes to attract right off. Of course, it is very difficult to get it right, but it may be a question of just sitting and waiting (or dancing and waiting) for the right person to come along, rather than targeting someone and frightening the wits out of them. The traditional advice is just be yourself, although you are allowed to experiment a little bit to find out what feels right for you!

Another thing which probably puts people off asking you to dance is when you form a little huddle with two or three of your closest friends, and other people feel they cannot break into your little group, especially if your backs are turned towards everyone else. If you would like someone to talk to you, or ask you to dance, it is a good idea to look at them (I don't mean stare hard – just a glance or two, and don't turn your back on them).

FURTHER ADVICE ON HOW TO GET TO DANCE WITH THE BOY/GIRL OF YOUR DREAMS

It is much more acceptable nowadays for girls to ask boys to dance (or ask them out), although the fear of rejection is just the same as it ever was for both sexes. Girls should actually have more insight these days into how it must have felt for a boy when it was solely his responsibility to ask a girl out or ask her to dance. You can't *make* someone go out with you or dance with you, but you can use subtle powers of persuasion. Don't ask me to explain 'subtle powers of persuasion', but I am sure they vary from person to person, including the way you look, talk, smile, dress, smell (sorry about this one), laugh, sing, tap-dance etc. etc. You can pay them a compliment or two, although you don't need to go over-the-top ("I just lurve the way your ears are glowing red and green in the disco lights!").

So, having used your subtle powers of persuasion and got the person to agree to have the next dance with you, you could sneak around to the DJ and request a slow smoochy number. Don't be too disappointed if the DJ (who may be a professional one or a parent or older sibling) turns out to have a warped sense of humour and you end up folk dancing.

PROBLEM THREE: When the 'disco dream' is over

● The scene

Amy has had a wonderful time, dancing with the boy she noticed standing alone at the school disco. Their eyes met across a crowded dance floor, the music swelled and they have spent the whole evening dancing together. Just before Amy's dad arrives to take Amy home, the boy, whose name is Mac (short for . . . Amy is not quite sure) asks Amy if she'd like to go for a walk with him tomorrow. Amy tells him her address, and feels that she is dancing on air all the

AMY AND MAC AT THE DISCO

way home. Her heart is still dancing at breakfast the next morning, and she spends ages getting ready.

At last the doorbell rings and it is Mac. Or is it? He doesn't look quite the same. He seems shorter and thinner (not Big Mac any more), and rather pale, with one or two spots. Amy has only been used to seeing him by strobe light, or in shades of red, green, blue and star-spangled silver by the disco lights, and he does not look so great by the cold light of day. However, appearances are not everything, and he and Amy go for their walk and try to find something to talk about. This is not so easy as Mac is only interested in football and racing cars, neither of which hold any particular appeal for Amy. She tells him of her dream of becoming a presenter on Breakfast Television, possibly as part of a

AMY AND MAC BY THE COLD LIGHT OF DAY

husband and wife team, and Mac begins to look slightly worried. It was all right as long as they were at the disco, because the loud music made conversation almost impossible, so they didn't have to bother.

● **The moral of this tale:** A mutual interest in dancing the night away to the Nut Girls and Dance-o-matic's Greatest Disco Hits doesn't constitute a whole relationship.

CHAPTER 7
Sport and Your Social Life

LET'S FACE IT. Life is NOT like an episode of Baywatch. Take a look at your friends and people you know. How many of them, yourself included, would look like they do in Baywatch, running along the beach, clad only in bikinis or swimming trunks? For a start, many of you would be out of breath after a few hundred metres, most would be pale and pimply (I'm sorry – I'm not saying that this applies to YOU in particular), and inevitably someone would trip and fall over. Apart from the fact that

OUCH!

OOF!

OW!

CRISPS

BRITISH BAYWATCH

the nearest beach to you is all rocks and pebbles, so most of you would be limping and, of course, it might well be raining. How about it, then? British Baywatch! Step forward, Spotty Sid and Flabby Fiona, for the first audition. No, perhaps not.

One admirable element in the great British character, however (and this is a gross generalisation, I know), is a tendency never to give up, even in the face of total defeat. There is also the ability to laugh at ourselves (sometimes) when we *are* beaten. If you are a good loser, then sports will be fun, and your enjoyment of sports can only enhance your social life. But if you are just in it to win, and totally flatten and annihilate the opposition, your fiercely competitive attitude is likely to alienate others. For instance, if you are the sort of person who shouts aggressively at the other members of the netball team if they drop the ball or put a foot wrong, you won't be very popular. And if you are a female javelin thrower determined to be the first woman to hurl your javelin right across the Channel as far as France, the boys are likely to run for their lives when they see you coming.

Similarly, if you are pathetic at sports, avoid over-competitive people and find some friends who just want to do sports for fun.

Some sports are more solitary than others. There is a book called *The Loneliness of the Long-distance Runner*. So you had better cross long-distance running off your list of sports which are good for your social life.

FACT — For boys especially, if you play sports well, especially the 'visible' sports like football, cricket and rugby, you will have little trouble finding a girl, unless you really aren't interested. You'll also have lots of mates. Being good at a sport also helps if you're a girl but it doesn't have quite the same pulling power.

PROBLEM ONE: Deciding which sport is best for you and your social life

● The scene - 1

Steve Cash has decided to take up surfing. He is fed up with looking pale and uninteresting, so he experiments with false tan and turns orange. Since he has recently dyed his hair green, he ends up looking like a giant carrot (looking like a giant carrot is not good for your social life). He carries a surfboard for effect, but since he lives sixty kilometres from the coast it is not very convincing — and it tends to knock people off the pavement. He also has difficulty manoeuvring it on to the school bus.

● A suggestion: Try a sport which is closer to home and more suited to the climate, local facilities, and so on.

● The scene -2

Angelica and Amy, who are great fans of Baywatch, decide to do some 'bodybuilding' exercises. They borrow a video by Mr Motivator with specially designed BLT exercises (Bums, Legs and Tums). They work out to this every day

MOVE THAT BODY!

after school in Mr and Mrs Toogood's living-room. Mr Motivator certainly manages to motivate Angelica, and she is motivated to go completely mad, swinging her arms and legs about in all directions until suddenly there is a terrific crash. Mrs Toogood's favourite vase has been knocked on to the floor and smashed into a thousand fragments. Mrs Toogood is not very happy about this, and Mr Motivator is turned off. Amy and Angelica feel de-motivated.

● **A suggestion:** It is probably better not to do athletic and other very vigorous sports inside your home, unless you are lucky enough to have a gymnasium, or you live in a barn, or somewhere very large (with not too many precious ornaments around). There is usually a leisure centre, or some kind of sporting complex, in the nearest large town, and this is obviously a better place to go if you wish to meet people and enjoy a better social life. You can go swimming or do aerobics or some other keep-fit class. This gives you a good excuse to parade around in a bikini, or a fashionable leotard and cycle shorts (if you are a girl, that is). Wearing the right sports gear makes you feel part of the crowd even if you don't do any sports! Parents are usually quite good about forking out money for these things as sports are always considered healthy and a good thing.

● The scene - 3

The lifeguards at the leisure centre are not quite up to Baywatch standards, but they are friendly, and they go to the same school as Angelica and Amy. One of them is quite good-looking. Angelica tries to attract his attention by performing graceful (she hopes) dives from the side of the pool. He doesn't seem to notice. She asks Amy to help her by working out a synchronised swimming routine.

"And don't forget to smile at him as we go underwater!" says Angelica. "Only you don't need to smile as much as I do," she adds, as an afterthought. "And then we've both got to turn upside-down and push our legs right up out of the water, so he can see them, right? And waggle them about a bit."

"Aren't we supposed to have some sort of little peg-thing on our noses?"

"I don't have any little peg-things! Anyway, do you think he'd fancy me if I had a little peg-thing stuck on the end of my nose?"

Amy and Angelica perform their routine. Amy holds her nose and tries to hold her breath long enough to push her legs out of the water. She manages to get them out of the water as far as her knees, and then feels herself sinking. Angelica falls sideways and pushes Amy deeper underwater. Amy is not a strong swimmer, and begins to panic. Her head bobs up briefly and then sinks below the surface again. Her arms thrash about wildly. Suddenly the good-looking lifeguard is there, rescuing her! He tows her to the side of the pool, and lifts her out.

"Are you OK?" he asks.

"Oh, yes!" replies Amy. "I'm fine, thanks. God, you saved my life!"

"Er . . . it was nothing. Don't mention it. Any time."

SYNCHRONISED SWIMMING

He wanders off to blow his whistle at some boys being stupid in the deep end. Angelica swims alongside Amy, and fixes her with a look (if looks could kill!). "You did that on purpose, didn't you?" she hisses.

● More suggestions:

1) Always take the proper safety precautions or wear the recommended safety gear when taking part in any kind of sport. Sitting for hours in the casualty department of the local hospital will do nothing for your social life.

2) If you are a proficient swimmer, you could train to be a lifeguard yourself, a good skill to know and a good way to meet people. The same applies to any other first-aid course.

3) It is debatable whether synchronised swimming is good for your social life or not.

4) Choose a sport which you are sure you are going to enjoy. Approach it in the right spirit. Otherwise you will simply shiver and look miserable, and this will not enhance your social life.

5) Don't push yourself to pursue a sport if you're feeling ill, or have an injury. Keep it in perspective. It should be fun.

PROBLEM TWO: Outside sports

● The scene

Amy asks for a football for her birthday. She and her friends like to play six-a-side football, with three boys and three girls in each team. They play this in the school playing-field, and also in the park near by.

On her birthday she invites Soumik, Baz, Grant (who is not keen on football, but likes Amy), Angelica and a friend called Jenny to come round, and then go out to play football.

⬤ **What Amy hopes will happen:** She hopes that a certain boy who she has noticed in the park nearly every day will see her playing football (and admire her nifty footwork and skilful ball control). She hopes that he will join in the game. Grant won't mind sitting on the sidelines, she is sure.

⬤ **What actually happens:** Amazingly, her wish comes true! (This is unheard of.) The boy, whose name is Scott (another Scott, not the same one . . . look, does it matter?), kicks the ball back to Amy when she has sent it in his direction 'by mistake'. Then he comes over.

"Mind if I join you?"

"No. I mean, no, I don't mind! Oh, God, you know what I mean. Do you?" Amy always talks too much when she is nervous. She feels quite trembly.

"I'll sit this one out," says Grant obligingly.

The game continues. Unfortunately, Amy trips over her best birthday long wrap-around skirt (not the best garment to play football in – but how do you balance playing football with attracting the boy of your dreams?) and falls over. Scott helps her up again, which is a not unpleasant experience. However, she feels a bit of a dork, covered in mud and grass stains.

They carry on playing. Amy decides that a good way to get close to Scott would be to tackle him when he next has the ball. Sadly, this turns out to be a bad idea when, unintentionally, she inflicts a very nasty kick right on Scott's shin.

"Oh, God, look – I'm really sorry!"

Scott is unable to speak. He limps away, and does not seem very keen to play football with Amy again.

⬤ **A suggestion:** Football is a wonderful game. It is great to play it with your friends. But it is not necessarily the path to romance. Of course, players traditionally embrace one another after someone has scored a goal. This is worth considering.

⬤ **Another suggestion:** Don't plot and scheme too much. Why not just relax and enjoy the game?

⬤ **And yet another suggestion:** How about 'armchair' sports? You could interpret this as 'sofa' sports. In other words, it is nice to sit beside someone you like and watch a sporting event on television. Less tiring, too (but not as healthy).

⬤ **A further thought:** As with any ball game, be careful where you play it. A smashed window or greenhouse or flattened prize plant will not help your social life. You will probably have to pay for repairs, and wave goodbye to the money you'd saved up for that special something.

THE SKATEBOARD/SNAKEBOARD/ ROLLERBLADE SCENE:

● What's good about skate-boarding/snakeboarding/rollerblading?

1) It is a good social activity. You meet other people, and you immediately have something in common, namely your skateboard etc.

2) If you are a girl, you can offer to time the boys. This is a good reason to hang out with the guys. Or you can put on your rollerblades and overtake them.

3) It is fun to have an admiring audience as you become a more experienced skateboarder.

● What's not so good about skateboarding/snakeboarding/rollerblading?

1) Be careful where you go skateboarding/snakeboarding/rollerblading. It would not be at all funny if you collided with someone and injured them.

2) It is not so good when you fall off and injure yourself.

MAKING IT BETTER:

● The scene

Scott has a skateboard. He has been practising his jumps in a quiet corner of the street where Amy lives. She has been watching him, timing him occasionally, and observing that from time to time, he falls off. She has an idea. She disappears into her house and returns with a complete first-aid kit, which she conceals behind the hedge. She waits for Scott to fall off again. She doesn't have to wait long. He falls forward and grazes the palms of his hands quite badly. Before he can pick himself up, Amy is at his side, tending his wounds.

"This might sting a little." She blasts his cuts and grazes with Savlon Antiseptic Wound Wash. Then she wipes a bit of grit away with a wad of cotton wool. The cotton wool sticks to the wound.

Scott is speechless. Tears come to his eyes. Amy is touched to know that he is so moved by her concern for him. "What did you have to do that for?" he blurts out at last. "It stings like . . ."

Amy is slightly taken aback. The words he uses seem a little uncalled for. She was only trying to help. Perhaps he is in pain. Still, it is nice to know that he will remember her for ever as a kind of Florence Nightingale. She notices, to her surprise, that he chooses not to go skate-boarding near her house again.

● **The moral of this tale:** If you fancy yourself as Florence Nightingale, it might be a good idea to go on a first-aid course first.

● **Suggestion:** It is a good idea to find out as much in advance as you can about any sport or activity you intend to take part in. For instance, you can join in a sponsored event (often a sporting one) for charity, and this is quite a good way of meeting people. You should be careful, however, of biting off more than you can chew. (This is particularly relevant advice, should you decide to embark on a sponsored fast. After the first few hours you will get a headache which will get steadily worse until you pass out completely from lack of food. This is not good for your social life.)

PROBLEM THREE: Doing sports with unflattering outfits

A WORD OF ADVICE – If you are a female rugby player, keeping your gumshield in at all times will not enhance your appearance or your social life. On the other hand, if you are a female rugby player, who is going to argue with you?

Seriously, some people look better in sports gear than others. If you are a girl and you happen to be a traditional British pear shape, then your tight-fitting cycle shorts will emphasise your rounded figure (all right, I mean the size of your bottom). Does this really matter? Frankly, no. Sports are meant to be fun. That's why you do them, not to look your best. Very few people look their best, for instance, in a pair of tracksuit trousers, sagging slightly at the knees. The whole point is to be as comfortable as possible so that you can move easily. If you enjoy a sport whole-heartedly, people won't really notice what you look like because they will be carried along by your enthusiasm and sense of fun. But if you stand around looking miserably self-conscious and uncomfortable in your hard hat and jodhpurs/judo suit/wet suit, flippers, mask and snorkel/knee pads, elbow pads, shin protectors, nose protector, and so on, everyone will notice how awkward you look.

So don't worry. Put on your goggles, strap on your helmet, pull on your waders, attach the safety harness – and go for it.

PROBLEM FOUR: When you're hopeless at sport (there's usually *something* you can do)

● The scene

Grant Toogood is not too good at sport. He enjoys watching it on television, but that is about as far as his interest goes. However, he has noticed that his friends are always going off on cycle rides together, while he is left behind. So he decides to revive his old bicycle, and take up cycling properly. This involves wearing a skin-tight all-in-one cycling suit and a helmet, which makes him look like a very tall, thin mushroom. He sets off down the road, wobbling slightly, and falls off on the grass verge in front of

FEELING A BIT STUPID IN YOUR BAGGY
OLD TRACKSUIT...

SUDDENLY YOU REALISE YOU'RE THE
HEIGHT OF FASHION!

SO WEAR WHAT FEELS RIGHT FOR <u>YOU</u>
AND WAIT FOR FASHION TO CATCH UP WITH
<u>YOU</u>!

HI, AMY— WANT TO COME FOR A CYCLE RIDE?

PRO

Amy's house. Amy comes out and helps him up.

"Thanks, Amy," he says. He leans forward to give her a kiss on the cheek, and succeeds in nearly knocking her out with his cycling helmet. "Er . . . sorry. Would you like to come for a cycle ride with me?"

● **What Amy is thinking:** No. No. I would feel a complete fool pedalling along behind a tall, thin mushroom-on-wheels. My friends might see me! Also, Grant is not fully in control of his legs, let alone his bicycle, and we are almost bound to have an accident.

● **What should Amy say?:** "Thanks, Grant, but my bicycle's broken." (Or any kind of excuse will do.)

● **Make an alternative suggestion:** "Why don't you go and get changed, and we could go for a walk together?" (There is no point in hurting someone's feelings if they are very obviously only doing a sport in order to find friends and company.)

Sport and Your Social Life

● **Fact:** Walking is very good exercise (and it is possible to dress more attractively to go walking than for most sports). You don't need special gear or equipment or any particular training or ability to do it. You can walk with friends, you can walk the dog, you can walk in the sunshine or in the rain, if you want to. You don't need to worry that someone is going to tell you you're not doing it right, or you've broken the rules, or that you're just hopeless at it. Walking is a sport that most of us do all the time, without even noticing. You can take this one step further (ha ha) if you like, and go hill-walking, depending on how energetic you are. You may even wish to invest in a pair of sturdy hiking boots, not to mention a Walkman. But always go in the company of a friend or friends, and keep to the beaten path. Better still, you could take part in an organised walk, or join the Ramblers' Association (you don't *have* to own an anorak, or a hat with a bobble on it). Always tell someone at home where you're going, and when you'll be back.

GOOD SOCIAL MOVE:
JOIN THE RAMBLERS' ASSOCIATION

CHAPTER 8
Mixing With Adults, and Other People's Parents

WHAT IS AN ADULT?

This is a difficult question to answer, because all adults are different. You may feel, at times, that they all have one thing in common: they think they know everything, and they like to tell you what you should or should not be saying/doing/thinking. You may feel this especially with your own parents, because you live together, and it is often difficult to avoid each other.

PROBLEM ONE: Your friends' parents (are they really always nicer than your own?)

The scene

Amy has had an argument with her parents, who have told her she can't go to a party organised by Steve and some of his friends, to be held at The Blue Porcupine, the trendiest night-spot in town (the only night-spot in town). She storms out of the house, calling out over her shoulder about how unfair they are, and how they just seem intent on ruining her life. They shout back at her that she ought to grow up a bit and that she could start by tidying her room. She goes to see Baz and his mother. She likes Baz's mother. Baz's mother pours her a glass of Coke. Amy considers the fact that at home she is not often allowed to drink Coke because her mother says it is bad for her teeth. Baz's mother, it would seem, is less concerned with dental hygiene, and more concerned with being kind and sympathetic.

● The score so far:

Baz's mum: 10

Mr and Mrs Average: 0

"How are you, Amy?" says Mrs Broke. "It's nice to see you."

"Oh, yes. It's nice to see you, too. I'm having a bit of a tough time at home."

"Oh, really? What's up? You know you can always come round here for a chat, don't you?"

● The score:

Baz's mum: 50

Mr and Mrs Average: 0

"By the way, Amy, I do like the way you've done your hair. It really suits your lovely personality. I often think, if I'd had a daughter, I would have liked one like you."

● The score:

Baz's mum: 6,000

Mr and Mrs Average: minus 40 (*They* were rude about her hair, and said it made her look like a scarecrow.)

* * *

But before Amy has a chance to explain to Mrs Broke how awful her parents are, Baz comes into the room. Suddenly Mrs Broke's whole attitude seems to change. She no longer seems kindly and sympathetic. She seems quite . . . what is the word? . . . cross.

"Basil! Will you please go and tidy your room immediately! I've been asking you to tidy it for days now, and you've taken absolutely no notice. I'm sure Amy keeps her room looking nice, don't you, dear?"

"Er . . ."

● **The score:**

Mrs Broke: back to zero

Mr and Mrs Average: also zero

"Oh, Mum! Look, I've got to practise for the gig at The Blue Porcupine. You know it's Steve's party. Are you going to be there, Amy?"

"Basil! Of course she isn't! I'm quite sure Amy's parents have more sense than to send Amy to one of Steve's parties. If I had a daughter who was the same age as Amy, I wouldn't allow her anywhere near The Blue Porcupine. They shouldn't let her in, anyway. She's under-age."

● **The final score:**

Mrs Broke: minus 10

Mr and Mrs Average: 0

● **The moral of this tale:** The grass is always greener on the other side.

PROBLEM TWO: Saying the wrong thing (whoops!)

● **The scene**

Soumik brings a friend called Mark home, and introduces Mark to his parents.

"It's nice to meet you, Mark," says Mrs Sen. "Have you known Soumik long?"

"Yeah, we've been mates for a long time. We hang out at the bus shelter every day."

"What bus shelter? Soumik does not travel by bus. Where is this bus shelter? Why do you need to hang around a bus shelter?"

"Er, the whole gang hangs out at the bus shelter."

"What gang? Soumik is not in a gang. I do not like the sound of this gang. I think we had better talk to Soumik."

● **What Soumik and Mark are both thinking:** Oh dear (or something like that). It is true that some parents are more easily upset or offended than others, but it is best to tread carefully, especially when you do not know them very well.

● **What Soumik can do to prevent Mark from putting his foot in it:** He can tell Mark a little bit about his parents before he introduces them. In particular, he can warn Mark about the things that worry them, such as strange people and unfamiliar situations. It is best to keep the conversation close to home and school and not to stray into unknown territory. When Mark is talking to Soumik's parents, he should keep an eye on Soumik in the background. If Soumik suddenly starts gesticulating and apparently doing a monkey impression, he is probably mouthing, "No! No!" meaning that Mark should stop what he's saying, and change the subject.

WHAT DO YOU DO IF YOU REALISE YOU'RE PUTTING YOUR FOOT IN IT?

1) Change the subject. A classic example is, "Oh, gosh, is that the time? I must fly!" Or a more charming one, "I like your curtains."

2) Have a terrible coughing fit. Someone will fetch you a glass of water, and you will be allowed to sit quietly, and say nothing.

SO WHAT *SHOULD* YOU SAY TO ADULTS?

1) If you give one word answers the whole time, you will sound rather rude. For example, they may ask you if you are enjoying school. A simple "No" may be true, but it is certainly an off-putting answer. Try to balance it by thinking of at least one thing that you enjoy about school (go on – think *hard*. Adults *like* enthusiasm). A truly inspired and winning answer to give to someone's parents might be to say that you've never been very keen on school but that you're enjoying it much more now that you're friends with their son/daughter.

2) Offer to help. If you have shared a meal at a friend's house, for example, offer to help with the washing-up. Say, "Is there anything I can do to help, Mrs Nesbitt?" (or whatever their name happens to be). Most adults find this approach irresistible. They will be utterly charmed and impressed by your polite and helpful attitude, probably contrasting it with the extreme unhelpfulness of their own offspring, and you will certainly be invited again. Hopefully they will be so bowled over by your generous offer to help that they will say something like, "Oh no, don't worry – you just go and enjoy yourself!"

OFFER TO HELP

3) "Please" and "Thank you" are important.

4) It is best to call your friend's parents Mr and Mrs Nesbitt (this is only an example, and you should of course substitute the appropriate surname). Wait to be invited to call them by their first names. When this happens, try to keep a straight face when they ask you to call them something wildly inappropriate (Fifi or Norm, or worse). If you really can't bring yourself to call them by their first names, you will just have to avoid calling them anything.

QUESTION: Are your parents really more embarrassing than your friends' parents?

● The scene - 1

Steve's dad has just bought a convertible Mercedes 360 SEL for his wife for her birthday. It is an unusual car because it is bright pink and has the number plate D OSH. Steve is embarrassed by the colour of the car, and by its number plate. Baz is fascinated, especially when Mrs Cash calls out to him, "Come on, Baz! Hop in, and I'll take you round the block!" She plays a Dr Drear tape at full volume on the car's stereo as they cruise past a little group of Baz's friends. Baz waves to them, and they cheer and wave back.

"Wow!" says Baz to Steve, when they get back. "Your mum's great! My mum would never do anything like that. She doesn't even have a car."

Steve just shakes his head sadly. "What a colour," is his only comment.

HOW EMBARRASSING IS MRS CASH?

● **Steve's opinion:** She is VERY EMBARRASSING.

● **Baz's opinion:** She's FAB. GREAT. GROOVY. WHACKY. Why is his own mother so BORING?

● **The scene - 2**

Mrs Broke has saved up enough money to buy herself a second-hand bicycle. It is a purple lady's bicycle, with basket and a cheerful little bell which Mrs Broke rings loudly as she rides past Baz, who is with a group of his friends, including Steve. She stops, and asks Baz if he would like a ride on the bicycle. Baz pretends not to hear.

"How about you, Steve?" says Mrs Broke. "Would you like a go on the bike?"

"Yeah! Why not?" says Steve. He goes for a ride, ringing the bell and pedalling furiously. His friends fall about laughing – apart from Baz, who does not laugh.

HOW EMBARRASSING IS MRS BROKE?

● **Baz's opinion:** TOTALLY, UTTERLY, HORRIBLY EMBARRASSING. SHE HAS COMPLETELY DESTROYED HIS STREET CRED.

● **Steve's opinion:** She is a LAUGH. She's GREAT. She is LOADS OF FUN. Why can't his own mother be more like her?

● **What is the answer to all this?:**
The fact is that ALL PARENTS ARE EMBARRASSING
if they are YOUR PARENTS. But remember: the grass is
always greener, and less embarrassing, on the other side.
Viewed from a distance parents can be quite FUNNY, and
the funny things they may do or say (or wear) occasionally
do not pose such a serious threat to your street cred as you
may think. Your friends are unlikely to let this affect the
way they feel about you. They probably feel the same
about their parents, and will be sympathetic.

GOOD THINGS ABOUT ADULTS AND OTHER PEOPLE'S PARENTS:

1) They can give you lifts to where you want to go, and
occasionally rescue you (for instance, if you are stranded at
a station/bus-stop with no money, and it is raining).
However, try not to use them as a taxi service. Always
thank them for coming out.

2) If you are interested in their son or daughter, they can
help you by telling you the sort of things their
son/daughter would like as a birthday or Christmas
present. If you are on friendly terms with the parent, they
can tell you all sorts of fascinating things you never knew
about their offspring. ("Scott just loves peanut butter and
sausage sandwiches." You can now rush out and get the
ingredients to make Scott a peanut butter and sausage
sandwich to end all peanut butter and sausage sandwiches.)

3) They can help organise and make possible all sorts of good things like parties, sleepovers, outings to the cinema, and so on.

4) Sometimes they can reassure you and help you understand why their son/daughter is apparently being unfriendly. ("Scott's always been a bit shy. He likes you, really. But he's had a hard time recently, and was bullied at the last school he was in.")

5) It is good to have somewhere to go and another friendly adult to talk to when your own parents are busy. You get to meet the whole family, and they introduce you to their friends and relations, which widens your social horizons.

CHAPTER 9
No Social Life

WHAT DO YOU DO IF YOU HAVE NO SOCIAL LIFE WHATSOEVER?

You may have just moved into the area, in which case you may not know your way around, and it's difficult to make friends when everyone has already formed their own friendships and close-knit groups. Or you may have fallen out with someone, and find yourself unexpectedly on your own (dumped). You don't feel part of it. You have no friends. But don't worry. There's lots you can do to put this situation right, soon you're going to be very busy, and you will probably end up longing for more time on your own.

PROBLEM ONE: Being approachable

● The scene

Everyone assumes that Steve is a cool and 'together' guy with loads of friends. He is always giving parties, and he seems to know everyone. However, he is usually on his own at parties, and no one seems to be particularly close to him. One evening he confides in Baz, who is a friend but finds Steve quite hard to get to know, that he is lonely. Baz is surprised, but then he feels touched that Steve has chosen to confide in him. A good first step towards forming a friendship is to reveal something about yourself that the other person would probably not have known just by looking at you (it's all right – this doesn't need to be something totally embarrassing. Mildly embarrassing will do). Of course, you need to get the balance right, because if you warble on and on endlessly about yourself, you will put the other person right off.

WHAT ELSE CAN STEVE DO TO LOOK APPROACHABLE?

1) Smile. This does not mean a ghastly fixed grin. Just a gentle lifting of the outer corners of the mouth will suffice (you can practise in a mirror). Don't overdo it. Raising your eyebrows at the same time until they disappear right under your hairline

GOOD SOCIAL MOVE:
SMILE!

will make you look completely mad. The best solution is probably to think of something or someone who you particularly like, and then the smile should come naturally. Remember: frowning uses thirty-two muscles in your face, whereas smiling uses fourteen. Why overwork?

2) You could wear a T-shirt emblazoned with a clear message that you want to be one of the crowd. There are all sorts of popular images or slogans which people will readily identify with. The right appearance probably helps to begin with. Later on, when you have made friends, you can give full vent to your individuality. If you do this initially you might put people off. (They cannot quite cope with your bright green hair and matching eyebrows.)

3) Equally, it's not a good idea to look too eager, or behave in a way that's too over-the-top. For instance, if you stride into a room full of people you don't know, go up to the first person you see and shout, "Hey, man, how you doin'? Gimme five!" you may be mistaken for a total prat. Similarly, grinning like an idiot, nodding furiously and agreeing with everyone, no matter what they are saying and regardless of whether they were actually talking to you anyway, will drive everyone round the bend. Don't try *too* hard.

PROBLEM TWO: Attracting someone's attention

● The scene

Amy likes Scott (a lot), but he is somewhat cool and distant towards her, even unfriendly. She would like to break the ice so that they can at least have a friendly conversation while waiting for the bus. What is the best and friendliest way of attracting (and holding) Scott's attention?

BAD WAYS TO ATTRACT SOMEONE'S ATTENTION:

1) Frequent clearing of the throat. The other person will assume that you have a nasty cough, and they will move away so they don't catch it. Frequent 'hem-hem-hemming' is also guaranteed to irritate rather than attract.

2) Showing off. Amy gets Angelica to sing loudly with her and perform a Nut Girls' dance routine close to where Scott is standing. This sort of thing is unlikely to impress. The other person is likely to look embarrassed/bored/fed up. They probably feel that you are only interested in being the centre of attention, and that it is impossible to have a normal conversation with you.

3) Avoid personal comments such as, "Did you know you've got a hole in your tights?", or "Wow! The sun's brought you out in loads of freckles! Or are they spots? I've got some really good spot cream you can borrow . . ." This sort of over-familiarity with someone you don't know very well will make you seem pushy and may cause offence. Don't say things like, "Oh, you poor thing, you look awful! Is there anything I can do?" It is likely the other person felt fine until you said this.

GOOD WAYS TO ATTRACT SOME-ONE'S ATTENTION:

1) "Hi, Scott, how are you?" A straightforward, friendly approach usually works well.

2) "You look great – that shirt really suits you." A little gentle flattery works well, but don't overdo it or you will embarrass them.

3) "I saw you at the leisure centre the other day. Do you go swimming a lot? It's supposed to be really good exercise, isn't it, so I'm thinking of going. What do you think of the pool?" Showing an interest in the other person and asking their opinion should result in a friendly conversation. It is fine to express your own opinions, as this will make you interesting, as long as you do not go in for overkill: "I hate swimming. It makes your eyes all red, and you smell of chlorine." Instead, mention something you *do* like. A cheerful and upbeat conversation is preferable to a series of moans, gripes and whinges.

4) Laugh at people's jokes even if they are not that funny but, again, don't force the laughter too much. Moderate laughter will do. You can practise this in your room, but not too loudly or you will worry your parents, or the dog. Laughter and smiling are good for you anyway, and help you live longer (and more happily).

PROBLEM THREE: Making an effort to make friends

● The scene

Soumik is bored with staying at home every night, and watching television. He wonders why he doesn't have more friends. The answer is, because he stays at home every night, watching television. He phones Baz, to tell him how bored he is. By some amazing coincidence, Baz is equally bored.

"Why don't we go to the youth club in New Borehampton?"

"Because it's boring."

What should they do? They should go and find out for themselves. If you dismiss everything as boring, you will inevitably turn into a very boring person yourself. It is necessary to make some kind of an effort to build a social life.

AT THE YOUTH CLUB:

Soumik and Baz are pleasantly surprised by the welcoming atmosphere. It's not at all boring. They play pool with some new friends, who then suggest a game of basketball (the youth club is held in quite a large hall). They are able to buy some crisps and a can of Coke, and the youth club leader is quite funny and easy to talk to. They listen to music, and play some arcade games, and then they sit down to watch part of a video, and have a chat with their new friends.

The good thing about any kind of club (whether it's a youth club/nature and conservation society/drama club, or other) is that you meet people with similar interests, so that you instantly have something in common to talk about.

AND THIS IS SIDNEY, ONE OF MY FAVOURITE AND FRIENDLIEST SPIDERS

GOOD SOCIAL MOVE:
JOIN A NATURE STUDY GROUP

You also get to see the same people again, on a regular basis, at weekly meetings perhaps, so you have the chance to get to know them quite well. Clubs and societies like this are usually well-organised and well-supervised, in a cheerful, informal way, so that you feel relaxed and able to enjoy yourself. You can find information about these clubs and societies and other social events in your local paper, or at the library, or at your school or sports centre. There is usually a notice-board which is worth looking at.

Alternatively, if you would rather not join a club or

society, there's nothing to stop you going along to the occasional exercise class or, if you have the money, you could go to a skating rink or swimming pool. You could step out on to the tennis courts or, if you're not feeling energetic, simply visit a café or go on a shopping expedition. You never know when you're going to find a friend (it may be the friend of a friend of a friend), but if you make the effort to go out to places where there are other teenagers, you're unlikely to be short of friends for long.

CONCLUSION – BALANCING IT ALL

Too many late nights and parties make you very tired, bad-tempered and give you bags under your eyes. The occasional early night is a good idea, especially when you have loads of schoolwork, exams, and so on. Do not be fooled by the person who seems to have a wild and wonderful social life the whole time – this person isn't real.

GOOD SOCIAL MOVE:

LOOK AFTER YOURSELF

(BREAKFAST IS AN IMPORTANT MEAL – EVEN
IF YOU EAT IT AT 2.30pm)

Or even if they are, they won't last long anyway. Everyone needs rest, time on their own, time to stand back and think about what is going on. You can just chill out and listen to music, maybe keep a diary of thoughts and feelings. Quiet days and evenings with one or two friends are more valuable than endless discos and parties with loud thumping music – and an equally thumping headache afterwards. Your social life should be fun and rewarding, not exhausting. You just need to get the balance right.

Angelica's idea of getting the balance right is to have a few friends (Amy and Jenny) for a sleepover, which means staying up all night talking and laughing. She then balances it by sleeping solidly for the rest of the weekend. Similarly, Baz goes to one of Steve's parties, and then balances it by sleeping for the whole of the following day. However, it does not go down too well with teachers at school if you catch up on lost sleep during their classes. If you find yourself doing this, then you have lost the necessary balance.

The whole of life, social and otherwise, is a bit of a balancing act, and it takes a certain amount of practise and experience before you get it right. Be prepared to take some advice from people who have been through it all themselves (parents). If you are willing to take some well-meant parental advice on board, your parents may feel encouraged to tell you about their own experiences when they were younger. When you have recovered from the shock of realising that your parents once had a social life, you will be able to have a good laugh with them at the complete mess they most probably made of it.